FUTURES—HUMAN AND DIVINE

FUTURES —HUMAN and DIVINE

by
Ted Peters

JOHN KNOX PRESS
ATLANTA

Library of Congress Cataloging in Publication Data

Peters, Ted., 1911–
    Futures, human and divine.

    Includes bibliographical references.
    1. Eschatology.   2. Forecasting.   3. Millennialism.
I. Title.
RT821.2.P45   236   77–79594
ISBN 0–8042–05741–4

© John Knox Press 1978

PREFACE

The future is an intrinsically moral concern. Thinking seriously about the future leads to making decisions in the present that help determine just what will actually happen. Decisions depend upon priorities; they depend upon our vision of what is important or most desirable. And the priorities we set emerge from the values we hold. Future thinking is indirectly and inevitably value thinking.

In thinking about Christian beliefs regarding the future, it is not enough to be concerned only with salvation after death. Doctrines such as heaven or hell, the eternal kingdom of God, resurrection of the dead, etc., have significance for the present life situation. They embody and express the values upon which people with religious faith set their priorities and make their decisions. Eschatology—the doctrine of last things—goes hand-in-hand with ethics. To think conscientiously about the future is to recognize that there is no escape from moral responsibility in the present.

This book is an attempt, first, to explore the intrinsically moral dimension to the widespread future consciousness in our world today. Second, it also attempts to suggest a philosophically sound foundation for a responsible Christian eschatology. And, third, it seeks to promote alliances between religious and nonreligious persons who are dedicated to making the future of this planet healthy, wholesome, and peaceful.

I dedicate this book to my three children: Paul, Kathy Kim, and Elizabeth Anne, and also to their future children, grandchildren, and greatgrandchildren, whom I will probably not live to see. May their future world in part be blessed by the decisions I am making and the actions I am taking in the present.

I want to thank my wife, Jenny, for her patience and encouragement during my years of research for this book and for the long hours she spent typing and retyping the manuscript. Such loving support is like God's grace, an undeserved gift to which only thanksgiving can be the appropriate response.

Ted Peters
New Orleans
September 20, 1977

CONTENTS

1
TOWARD THE YEAR 2000

It is a curious thing that as we approach the year 2000 both the secular and scientific communities are taking a millennialist perspective. "Millennialism" traditionally referred to the doctrines surrounding the 1000-year reign of Christ foretold in the book of Revelation, and as the year A.D. 1000 approached there were great religious stirrings in medieval Europe over what this would mean. Today the secular and scientific communities are just as concerned about the year 2000. We have a flood of books with titles such as *Toward the Year 2000* and *Mankind 2000*. There are conferences on "Humanity in the Year 2000"; the future of this industry or that "in the year 2000" is now a standard boardroom topic; and cities such as Atlanta have done self-studies with titles like *Atlanta 2000*. The theme for the Second General Assembly of the World Future Society held in Washington in 1975 was "The Next Twenty-Five Years." Of course, many are looking beyond the year 2000; they seek to have 2020 vision or better.

All this has given rise to a new academic profession: namely, futurology. Futurology is the science that seeks to understand the future and to provide the tools whereby humans can obtain greater control over their own destiny. Alvin Toffler uses the term "futurist" to denote "a growing school of social critics, scientists, philosophers, planners, and others who concern themselves with the alternatives facing man as the human race collides with an onrushing future."[1]

Why all the concern over what will happen in the next few

decades? The ecology-minded sociologist John McHale says, "The next fifty years may be the most crucial in all of man's history."[2] Why?

The major concern seems to be this: the surface of our planet is exploding with the development of science and technology, but it is a random and uncoordinated growth which lacks orientation and direction. Technology has given us the power to feed all the earth's peoples but only a third are getting the food; advances in industry and medical care have given us the ability to increase our population to 15 billion in the next half-century but the earth's natural resources are unable to feed them; mass communications have become so sophisticated we will soon be able to link everyone in the world through electronics, but this ability also provides means for total surveillance and control of people by a ruthless government; biomedical research will soon give us the ability to predetermine a child's sex, physical features, and intelligence, and even bring it to birth outside the mother's womb, but we do not know who should decide when, where, or for what purpose. In short, the responsibilities of our scientific future are too big for the scientist to shoulder alone. Scientifically oriented futurists can forecast the alternatives for the future, but someone must decide which future humanity will have. Such decisions will depend on our values; the concerns of human values can no longer leave science to go it alone. John McHale writes:

> The material control of future possibilities comes largely through the development of science and technology which have been traditionally value-free agencies. But the present range and scale of our actions and their consequences require increasing value commitments to specifically preferred and possible futures in human terms.[3]

Parallel to and somewhat predating the rise of the futurist movement in the secular and scientific world, there has been a revival of future consciousness among Christians. In 1968 the World Council of Churches launched a five-year study program on "The Future of Man and Society in a World of Science-Based Technology." The title reveals the aim of promoting dialogue between secular and religious perspectives on the future. In addition, two of the presently dominant schools of academic religious thought are the Theology of Hope and the Theology of Liberation, both future-oriented. The more conservative wing of Protestantism is experiencing a revival of millennialist thinking with the flood of popular books by Hal Lindsey and attendance at such movies as *The Omen*.

The Bible itself is a future-oriented book; the people of God always live in memory *and* anticipation. From the time of God's promise to Abraham in Genesis 12, the prophets of God were constantly projecting a new future to be brought about by both God and humanity. Their image of that future would change from time to time, but there was always some image presenting the ideal goals God hoped to fulfill in his future kingdom. Those ideal goals always stood in judgment over present inadequacies, but, when accompanied with confidence in God's grace, they also served to inspire committed human action toward realizing them.

FUTURE CONSCIOUSNESS

Our Western civilization has long been imbued with a general orientation toward the future; and the present period is witnessing an especially acute epidemic of future consciousness. And despite the variety of personal and academic backgrounds of the growing number of professional futurists, they all seem to be in agreement on one point, namely, if we are to have a future at all, we must make a radical change in the values that orient the economic and social systems of the West. Our value system is now threatening humanity —through nuclear war, pollution of the biosphere, resource depletion, and starvation. And what is the *central* value of our value system? That value is nothing short of *selfishness.* Using other more erudite language, social scientists and political dissidents have discovered that selfishness is creating problems for humanity, and that what we need as a human race is to embrace such values as prudence, sharing of one's wealth, and respectful concern for both nature and neighbors.

Economist Robert Theobald describes the problem as competition and the win-lose mentality.

> We need to understand that the competitive model of
> the last two centuries—striving against others, trying to
> get to the top of the heap whatever the cost—is no
> longer feasible or desirable. The persistence of this
> model is now the prime reason why we cannot develop
> our own lives in sensible, valuable ways.[4]

Georgetown University political scientist Victor Ferkiss labels
the problem "liberalism" and calls his solution "ecological humanism."

> The essence of humanity's current crisis is that we have
> allowed our collective destiny to be determined by the
> political philosophy usually called liberalism, which
> holds that the prime purpose of human society is to
> encourage individual self-aggrandisement.[5]

What are the "new" values we must embrace in order to preserve the ecosphere and sociosphere for our grandchildren? Futurists explain that we need to value humanity more than the machine,
to value nature in its own right rather than as a mere object for our
manipulation, to value community needs over individual desires, to
value sharing food with the hungry over making a profit for ourselves, to be imbued with world-concern rather than mere self-
concern. We are being urged to replace individual selfishness with
a concern for the welfare of all.

I argue that what is being advocated here is more than simply
social science. Although the term is out of vogue in certain quarters
of humanistic parlance, I suggest that what we have here are genuinely "religious" concerns. One would have to be grossly naive
about the history of Western culture to have overlooked the continuing *religious* concern with human selfishness. Selfishness has long
been understood to be the root cause of tragedy. It always threatens self-destruction, and the particularly Christian motif of divine
forgiveness issuing in the saints' self-giving love for humans and
nature has been proposed as the cure. The vocabulary may have
changed since the Enlightenment, but the issue itself predates the
modern era by millennia.

It is interesting that the solutions being proposed are dubbed
"radically new." Radical they are, but new they are not. Having

become worshipers of the triumphs of modern technological and democratic civilization, we are so in the habit of believing ourselves superior to all previous periods that we easily overlook some of the virtues of the Middle Ages. The medieval world believed selfishness was a sin to be condemned, not a right to be exercised through the exploitation of nature and the marketplace. God had given the earth to humanity as a whole, and under human tutelage nature was to be nurtured and enjoyed. Even Lynn White, in an article otherwise critical of Christianity, "The Historical Roots of Our Ecological Crisis,"[6] goes to the medieval saint, Francis of Assisi—who believed in the equality of all nature's creatures rather than the supremacy of humans—for an ideological model for contemporary ecology.

Private property in the Middle Ages could be justified as a social convenience in allocating resources and responsibilities, but all ownership was seen as stewardship of what really belonged to God. Greed was condemned as a vice. Thomas Aquinas held that if a starving man were forced to steal from a rich man in order to survive, it would not be counted a sin; the superfluities of the rich really belonged to the poor.

Hence, it seems that Christendom's medieval teaching could possibly provide key elements in the value system we need for meeting our present crisis. It is doubtful, however, that anyone will seriously consider retrieving medieval Christianity, because the notion of calling back something from the past is itself repugnant to future-oriented moderns. The solution to our crisis must be a new one; an old one just will not do. We are told that Enlightenment humanism and the rise of technological civilization have freed us from the Middle Ages forever; how shattering it would be to interpret modernity as a fall from something higher rather than as a rise above something inferior! Consequently, even our futurists' vision is one-directional, looking toward the future, which itself is expected to provide the resources to make our future a good one. Rather than challenge this belief, I will be content to point it out and then accompany other futurists in their attempt to find in the vision of the future itself the resources to meet our present crisis. But as a Christian theologian, I can draw upon a broader and more inclusive tradition of futuristic thinking than is possible for those who restrict themselves to the social sciences and secular humanism.

The purpose of this book then is twofold: first, to show that future consciousness itself is an intensely religious phenomenon; and, second, to present one view of Christian eschatology that securely anchors a holistic value system in the future of God.

Future consciousness is religious. By this I mean two things. First, in some cases it is explicitly religious because overtly religious groups from time to time express a distinctive concern for the future. Religious millennialists, for example, are anxiously awaiting the second coming of Christ with bumper-stickers such as "Guess Who's Coming Again?" Second, there are implicit religious dimensions to much of even avowedly secular futuristic thinking.

This second and more-difficult-to-appraise dimension—the understanding of secular future consciousness as implicitly religious—demands a principle of interpretation. The method I intend to use for studying this dimension is a *hermeneutic of culture.* The term "hermeneutic" originally referred to the theory and method for interpreting literary texts. Literature, of course, is one form of cultural expression. Music, art, technology, political habits, language, etc., are also means whereby a given culture objectifies its beliefs, goals, religious orientation, understanding of reality, and sensitivity to the human situation. Recently the term "hermeneutic" has been applied to the interpretation not only of literature but of music, art, and all other forms of cultural self-expression.

The depth and inner dynamic of any given culture is its religion, according to scholars in the tradition of Paul Tillich. A hermeneutic of culture proposes to interpret cultural phenomena in such a way as to bring that depth and dynamic into clearer focus. This method is quite akin to Langdon Gilkey's "hermeneutic of secular experience." Gilkey uses the term "hermeneutic" drawn from Martin Heidegger's phenomenology because it "seeks to interpret the latent *meanings,* i. e., unveil the implicit structures, of man's being in the world"; it attempts to uncover the religious dimensions of human concerns even when they are covered over by secular rhetoric.[7]

A close examination of how even secularists grapple with the issues confronting our future reveals that *ultimate* concerns predominate. Most future-oriented thinking at present is not preoccupied with the type of mascara to be donned by the twenty-first-century woman or whether the flush toilet will become obsolete. Rather, it is dominated by ultimate questions: Will the human race survive? If the human race does survive, will it still be human? Will it succumb to the hegemony of the machine? Will it be so altered by bio-engineering that it will become a superhuman species? These questions seem to orbit the nuclear problem: if it is true that we will determine our tomorrow by the decisions we make or do not make today, then which vision of what people ought ultimately to be do we draw on for setting our priorities? For it is the vision of what human life ultimately should be in the future that determines the things we value and how we set our priorities in the present.

Future consciousness plunges consistently into questions regarding ultimate values—and this makes it intrinsically religious. "Religion, in the largest and most basic sense of the word, is ultimate concern," wrote Paul Tillich.[8] The functional role of religion in culture and personal existence is to orient and ground our fundamental values. Some philosophers believe religion is basically a way of valuing—or better, the experience of being grasped by a sense of worth that transcends all other values. Frederick Ferré says, "Religion is one's way of valuing most comprehensively and intensively."[9]

The future itself, even in secular circles, seems to take on many of the qualities we ordinarily ascribe to the divine: mystery, transcendence, an extra-human power to save us, and an ability to determine the ultimate value or non-value of anything that exists in the present. It is this broad definition of religion as ultimate concern which I intend to use here, rather than the narrower notion of religion usually associated with organized churches and theological vocabulary. In this sense a church council meeting or a denominational convention that swims through oceans of debate over menus and budgetary trivia is as nonreligious as a cocktail party at the neighborhood bordello. On the other side, the agnostic sigh, "I wonder what it all means?" is a vital religious concern regardless of how it is answered.

We need a hermeneutic of future consciousness, but admittedly the vantage point from which to launch an interpretation cannot be

the future itself. It must be the present or the past. We can only view
the future in terms of the present, and the present is in strong
measure a product of the past.

Traditionally, orthodox Christian theology grounded its belief in
a *past* event. That event was the career of Jesus. But it was never
really thought of as strictly a *passed* event; it was always living in
the present. To preach Jesus crucified was simultaneously to convict
the listener of his or her own sin; to retell the story of Jesus' Easter
resurrection was all that was necessary to inspire hope and confidence in our own victory over death. Orthodoxy drew no line
between past and present when it came to understanding the operations of God's grace in human history; both were assumed to be
important. However, this somewhat naive marriage of the past and
present was rent asunder in the nineteenth century with the development of historical-critical consciousness. By historical-critical consciousness I mean the awareness that the story of Jesus (as well as
all other ancient accounts) had a meaning for its own time and place.
This meaning was different from the meaning it has for us, because
we live in a different historical period or context. The thought-world
of the Bible is different from ours. Hence, to understand the Bible
we need to make an effort toward understanding the world view in
which it was first written and to which it first attempted to speak.
We simply cannot make direct or literal application of the Bible to
the present.

Historical-critical consciousness increased the distance between
past and present. The more our story of Jesus and other Biblical
episodes became objects of historical study, the more divorced they
became from present-day lived experience. The contrast between
a dead past and a living present became more vivid. Eventually
Christian faith seemed to lose its grounding in the past events
recorded in Scripture. Orthodoxy gave way to Liberal theology and
then to Neo-orthodox and Existentialist theology.

Neo-orthodox theology sought to reground faith in the present, independent of the conclusions of historical research. Neo-
orthodox theologians contended that in today's proclamation of
Jesus' crucifixion and resurrection God works *now* to transform the
hearer. The *Word* of God in the present is distinguished from the

words of the Bible written in the past. God's Word works now by challenging us to make a decision, to throw off our past and to open ourselves to a new and different future. Paul Tillich says we need only the "biblical picture" of the Christ—not the real Jesus of past history—for God to work in our life existentially.[10] Rudolf Bultmann goes further, saying even the picture of Jesus indicates too much memory; God's Word works in the instant that it is preached.

And in certain respects the future is also lost. Bultmann redefines "eschatology" so that it no longer refers to a cosmic future event but to a present individual experience of decision-making.[11] Karl Barth's interpretation of Easter as the eternal presence of God within human time leads him to conclude that this event has no future eschatological significance at all.[12] For the Neo-orthodox, then, both past and future seem to be collapsed into the present.

But can the present interpret itself? No, I do not think so. The present is in the same position that we find the future. We can interpret the meaning of one situation only by comparing it with another, by seeing it within a wider context. I suspect it would be difficult to know what a fishbowl looks like if you always had to live inside it. Unless you can step out of it and view it in relation to other items in the room you cannot ascertain its true shape and proportions.

The Neo-orthodox are kidding themselves when they advocate total reliance upon the present. They understand the workings of God now only on the basis of comparing what they presently observe with what God did in the past as reported by Scripture. We need the past to understand the present, and only the historian can give it to us. Without this hermeneutical vantage point, we would have simply brute experience without being able to recognize that the same "god" is at work here and now as was at work in Jesus Christ. Brute experience has no meaning at all. It must be seen always in its wider context, i.e., the context of past tradition and future expectation, before it has meaning. Overemphasis on the present existential moment leads to nihilism. Thus, despite the problems created by historical-critical consciousness, we must not divorce ourselves too quickly from our roots in the past.

This conviction has helped to precipitate a renewed concern for

hermeneutics in Christian theology in the past two decades. Her-
meneuts recognize that the past influences the present, and our past
includes the Bible plus all the interpretations of the Bible down to
the present day. We need to understand the future in terms of this
past. "The task of the hermeneutical disciplines," writes Wolfhart
Pannenberg, "is to interpret the transmitted material from the past
in relation to the future, to the extent that the latter forms the
horizon of present understanding, so that the importance of the past
for the present with regard to its future becomes intelligible."[13]

In this book I will attempt to develop a hermeneutic of future
consciousness by making reference to one significant past event,
namely, the Easter resurrection of Jesus, and one significant event
promised for the future, namely, the advent of the kingdom of God.
Once we have drawn a connection between past and future in terms
of these two events, I believe we will have a perspective for interpreting the meaning of the present. It is finally the dynamic relationship between future and present that will occupy us in our treatment
of future consciousness. But first let's look at the nature of current
future consciousness, so that what I say theologically will be in
dialogue with secular ways of looking at the future.

SOME STRUCTURAL ELEMENTS IN FUTURE CONSCIOUSNESS

The first element in the structure of future consciousness is dissatisfaction with the present combined with hope for the new. The
present stands under judgment: condemned to death in hopes of
resurrection to a new and better tomorrow. In Charles Reich's *The
Greening of America,* the selfishness that leads to a loss of self in
Consciousness II (Ferkiss: "liberalism") is condemned in favor of an
optimistic forecast for Consciousness III, which, Reich says, "promises a higher reason, a more human community, and a new and
liberated individual. Its ultimate creation will be a new and enduring
wholeness and beauty—a renewed relationship of man to himself,
to other men, to society, to nature, and to the land."[14] Theologians
of hope and liberation are similarly dissatisfied with the present.
They hope for a new future in which people will become free from
the oppressions of the present. Carl Braaten, for example, believes
Christianity is a "conspiracy for freedom."[15] And, similarly, James

Cone condemns present oppression with confidence in the future of liberation because of the hope produced by God's victory in raising Christ from the grave.[16]

Not only is the present situation condemned; often present trends are feared as well. The famous Club of Rome study *The Limits to Growth* argues dramatically that if present trends in population growth, resource use, and pollution continue unabated, then we will meet a worldwide calamity just beyond the year 2000.[17] This draws our attention to a second and related element in the structure of future consciousness: namely, the feeling that the power of change itself is beyond human control. Alvin Toffler titled his best-selling book *Future Shock* in order to express the feeling that we are being overwhelmed by change.[18] There is dissatisfaction, then, not only with the way the present is but also with the prospect that the changes operating in the present may continue and ruin the future too. Here, in non-theological language, is our need for redemption expressing itself. Caught in the eddy of demonic forces in the present, we hope for rescue and renewal in the future.

A third element in secular future consciousness presumes that we must rely upon humanity to rescue itself. To overcome the powers determining the present state of affairs and trends, all we need do is properly diagnose the source of our ills and then decide to make the plans necessary to cure them. Furthermore, as humanists the futurists call upon us with great moral fervor to make the *right* decisions. The Club of Rome argues that unless we human beings decide how we want to limit our own growth, nature will do it for us. Gordon Rattray Taylor reports that biomedical technology is on the verge of predetermining the sex and intelligence of children before birth and that by 1985 science may have perfected the art of cloning—the reproduction of an infinite number of genetically identical people from the cells of one person. Taylor implores us not to simply let technology roll along its own path but to decide how and what is to be done with these newfound powers over human evolution.[19] Future consciousness inevitably leads to moral consciousness. If we are to have a truly "human" future, then we humans must make the moral decisions necessary to take control over our destiny. And the theology of the world of Johannes B. Metz advocates that Christians unite with other humanists in the technological, scientific, and political arenas where planning for the future is done.[20]

A fourth element in modern future consciousness is the sense of the ultimate destiny of all humanity. We are becoming a single planetary society. Electronic communications and international trade have brought peoples with the most diverse cultures into a kind of "globe-think." On the questions of growth in population, pollution, and resource depletion, the Club of Rome used a world model because they believed the future of the whole world is at stake. The questions about the future now being asked are about the survival of the entire human race. In the words of R. Buckminster Fuller, it is a question of "utopia or oblivion."[21]

These are ultimate concerns. The concern for the very survival of the race is not a penultimate concern, not subordinate to other more important things. Furthermore, as futurists project visions of the kind of utopia they desire in place of oblivion—such as Reich's Consciousness III—they sound a good deal like those who project the Christian vision of the kingdom of God.

FUTUROLOGY AND ESCHATOLOGY

Although phenomenologically there seems to be a good deal in common between secular future consciousness and avowedly religious or theological reflections upon it, there are some significant differences. These differences can be clarified by comparing pairs of words such as *futurology* and *eschatology, futurum* and *adventus,* and *becoming* and *coming.* Like other terms ending in -ology, *futurology* is the study of the future. *Eschatology* is the study of the *ta eschata,* coming from the Greek, meaning "the last things." Each study approaches the one future from different directions: futurology extrapolates from past and present trends towards the near future, whereas Christian eschatology begins with what has been prophesied about God's final future and then approaches the present.

These two approaches can be distinguished by the Latin terms *futurum* and *adventus. Futurum* is the future actualization of potentialities already existing within things. An oak tree is the acorn's *futurum.* The future is understood as simply the growth, development, maturation, or fruition of forces or trends already at work in the present. *Adventus,* in contrast, is the appearance of something new. It is a first. It is a future that can be anticipated or hoped for, but its arrival is not dependent only upon present potentialities. It cannot be understood through projections based upon present trends.

Secular futurology begins with an examination of present trends in human history—and it may be a very scientific examination—and then through extrapolation projects what may or may not happen if one or another trend gains dominance. It projects what may *become* the future. Any transformation of the present world will have to be achieved with only the resources and potentialities that already exist. Christian eschatology, on the other hand, awaits the advent of God's final kingdom, i.e., the *coming* of "a new heaven and a new earth." Eschatology hopes for a new reality, a God-provided transformation and new creation of humanity and our environment. Carl Braaten states it: "A crucial difference between secular futurology and Christian eschatology is this: the future in secular futurology is *reached* by a process of the world's *becoming.* The future in Christian eschatology *arrives* by the *coming* of God's kingdom. The one is a *becoming,* the other a *coming.*"[22]

The distinction between *futurum* and *adventus* is not merely the arbitrary construction of theologians invented to make room for eschatology. Applying our hermeneutic to the experience of future consciousness, we see that *adventus* is universally the deeper and more genuine apprehension of what the future is. There is something about *adventus* that is mysterious; it is not subject to complete analysis and calculation on the basis of present reality. *Futurum* is. And because *futurum* projects what is to come as the concrete extension of what is already determined, it really understands the future only as a quality of the present. But the distinctive nature of the future that really grips our imaginations is the quality of mystery, the uncertainty, the question of whether our plans may not yet be thwarted by some unpredictable factor or event. The prominent Roman Catholic theologian Karl Rahner writes:

> The future is that to which we ourselves cannot reach out, but which rather comes to us of itself—when it decides to—and with which we have to deal, strangely, precisely on *these* terms. . . . It is that which cannot be

controlled or calculated, which again and again wells
up and breaks through the most precise calculations of
the future, makes room for them and yet at the same time
always makes them provisional and doubtful of accom-
plishment.[23]

Although scientific futurology is an attempt to control the future
using calculations and plans based upon the present, the sense of
the future as *adventus* still makes itself felt and is expressed in the
concept of contingency. In the process of forecasting which one of
the present trends is likely to be dominant in the years to come,
scientific futurology finds itself in the position of projecting many
different potential futures contingent upon which one people decide
to actualize. The alternative futures have been dubbed "futuribles"
by the French political economist Bertrand de Jouvenel. Hence,
scientific futurology does not *predict* the future, because what will
in fact take place depends so much on what people will decide to
do. No one could have predicted in advance the Watergate debacle because the actual course of events was contingent on the
decisions and actions of certain individuals who could have decided
otherwise. Futurists make *forecasts,* not predictions. Forecasting
extrapolates from the regularities in trends but always with an eye
to the contingency factors. Forecasting incorporates the use of
algorithms, or decision-rules, which project that futurible *A* will probably occur if a certain decision is made, but futurible *B* will probably
occur if the decision is not made.

Hence, futurology only helps us to understand the possibilities
of the future; it does not actualize them. The futurists provide us with
alternatives of what *could* happen in the future; they do not make
unconditional predictions. Another ingredient is necessary before
we move from the possibilities envisioned now to the actualized
future. That element is human *decision* and the actions that follow
from it. The decisions we make or do not make now, the futurists
tell us, will determine the actual future we will have. Futurology tells
us what *can* happen, but it presumes that only human decision can
make it happen for the good.

VALUES AND ESCHATOLOGY

In this way the concerns of the forecasters go beyond the mere call to scientific responsibility. The generally accepted view of the scientist's responsibility is to maintain dispassionate objectivity with regard to the facts, and that means that scientists must refrain from imposing any of their "personal values" into the research. In the case of the scientific futurists, however, many of them are not content to merely present the futuribles their research has uncovered. Rather, after presenting the alternative futures which are possible they challenge us to decide on behalf of one or another.

Indeed, future consciousness almost inevitably leads beyond forecasts into value concerns. It has been forecasted, for example, that according to present rates of use our planet will be exhausted of its supply of unrenewable natural resources somewhere within the twenty-first century unless, of course, we decide upon a plan of conservation and develop a "soft technology" which would greatly lengthen the time of resource availability. It seems that the very forecasting of tuturibles intensifies our awareness of the contingency factors and challenges us in the area of decision-making. But how should we make these decisions? That is the extra-scientific question to which futurology inevitably leads.

Decision-making is done according to one's priorities, and priorities emerge out of one's value system. What we value most we place on our list as top priority. Questions about values belong to the sphere of the philosopher or the theologian, not the scientist, at least insofar as the field of science is commonly understood. Of course, the work of the philosopher or theologian ought to be done in tandem with that of the scientific futurist. Theology in particular has on occasion spun out lengthy theories about celestial realities that ignored the plain facts, with the consequence that theology was often dismissed as irrelevant to the genuine human predicament. It is hoped that the present book will not make that mistake. If theologians have any vision of God's intended destiny for humans, they can offer a basic point of departure for developing a system of values and priorities capable of meeting the challenges to decision-making and planning presented by the scientific forecasting of alternative futures. If you know what is ultimately important, you have taken the first step toward making the appropriate decision. What is important is God's ultimate intention for the future of humankind. God's intended future is the criterion of values according to which we set our priorities.

What *is* the promised destiny for humanity according to Christian eschatology? Eschatology usually concerns itself with judgment, resurrection of the dead, and the kingdom of God. Judgment means the present is unworthy of everlasting continuance. This leads to death and resurrection. The second tree in the garden of Eden, besides the tree of the knowledge of good and evil, was the tree of life. God expelled Adam and Eve from the garden before they could eat fruit from the tree of life. Should they have eaten of the tree of life, they would have lived forever in their sinful state. Keeping them from continuing forever on their present path and allowing them to die was an act of God's grace, because death to our present state of existence is a necessary door to a new and better one. Judgment against the present is the prerequisite for resurrection to a new future.

Resurrection is the heart of Christian eschatology. However, it is not resurrection merely in the sense of resuscitating corpses, of returning people to their everyday pattern of living. It is rather transformation. Jesus' resurrection on Easter is the model of the resurrection which a renewed and transformed humanity will enjoy in the future kingdom of God. The resurrection promised us is a transformation from the present eon to the new creation, and death to the old is the door. In the words of Paul, what is sown perishable will be raised imperishable, what is sown in dishonor will be raised in glory, what is sown in weakness will be raised in power, what is sown a physical body will be raised a spiritual body (1 Cor. 15:42—44).

As the concept of resurrection signifies God's intention to transform the individual human being, so also the concept of the kingdom of God signifies the transformation of society and nature. The term "kingdom" refers to the reign or lordship of God, to that time when the will of God becomes actualized. Eschatology does not only deliberate over salvation for the individual; it is also concerned to project a final conclusion to world history and the reconstitution of human society on new terms.

The Bible promises a transformed humanity which has overcome the alienation of individuals from each other and from God. It is the promise of Micah 4:3 as inscribed on the cornerstone of the United Nations:

> they shall beat their swords into plowshares,
> and their spears into pruning hooks;
> nation shall not lift up sword against nation,
> neither shall they learn war any more.

The unity of person with person is simultaneously a unity all will share with God. When Jeremiah prophesies a "new covenant," God says, "I will put my law within them, and I will write it upon their hearts." (Jer. 31:33) God's law, according to Jesus, is that we love God and one another (Matt. 22:37—40). What this means is that humanity as we now know it does not love God and neighbor, otherwise the law would not appear to us as outside of us. It is because we do not in fact love one another that the injunction to do so stands over against us as an ethical demand. It is our selfishness that necessitates moral law and alienates us from God; when love is perfect there is no need for moral laws and God is at home.

The eschatological new humanity will no longer need morality, nor organized religion either, for that matter. Religion exists only because all of us are alienated from God. In the "New Jerusalem" pictured by the book of Revelation there will be no temple where people go to worship God; if God's law is written upon the citizens' hearts, then he is everywhere present. Perhaps ironically both humanists and Christians can agree that when humanity truly "comes of age" we will be beyond institutional religion.

Alienation and conflict within nature will also be overcome. Despite the romantic interpretations of mother nature fawning delicately over her creatures which make up the imagery of some ecological rhetoric, mother nature can really be a "bitch." Mother nature may have created life, but she is also careless about life. Her creatures exist by eating one another. Small fish eat plankton and then big fish eat the small fish right on up the food chain. Bucks fight

each other to the death to mate with a particular doe and perpetu-
ate the herd of deer. The messianic prophecy of Isaiah, however,
looks forward to the divine kingdom in the future when "the wolf
shall dwell with the lamb, and the leopard shall lie down with the
kid, and the calf and the lion and the fatling together." (Isa. 11:6)

Victor Ferkiss and dozens of secular and Christian futurists alike
are correct in their analysis of our present problem, namely, that
human selfishness—concretely expressed in our values and institutions as the desire to maximally exploit nature and other people—
is leading us toward self-destruction. When the desire for self-
fulfillment is understood as competition rather than cooperation, as
individual salvation at the possible expense of other individuals and
the whole, then when the available goods reach their finite limit
every victory necessitates a loss. People must win and nature lose;
and one person must win while another person loses. Selfishness
alienates a person from other people, from nature, and from God.

Futurists want a cure for selfishness. They judge it as wrong; they
want to see it die and to see a new humanity, imbued with the values
of an ecological humanism, resurrect itself. Their hope is in *futurum*,
not *adventus*. They would like to see present selfish humanity suddenly re-create itself. Wouldn't we all? But as the prophet Jeremiah
asked (Jer. 13:23), can a leopard change its spots? Can humanity
with its history of selfishness accomplish this change alone?

Christian eschatology holds a vision of the ultimate future that
basically endorses what secular humanists want to see occur. Both
seek a world that is more humane, more just, more peaceful, more
egalitarian, more free from the destructive consequences of unmiti-
gated egoism. A society in which the members would have the law
of God "written on their hearts" would embrace harmony and
eschew exploitive competition. This future is the ground of value and
source of our priorities for many in both religious and nonreligious
groups.

Both secular and Christian futurists hold up this vision of what can
or will be in the future in order to awaken our sense of moral
responsibility. They challenge us to come out in support of this vision
and to take action now to eventually bring it to pass. Our image
of this futurible presents us with our moral obligation; it is God's law

standing over us and judging our present as deserving of death on behalf of a new resurrection.

The key difference between futurology and eschatology on this score is the difference between *futurum* and *adventus,* between law and gospel. Eschatology senses the need to rely on the power of the future *over against* the present in order to transform selfishness into love. Should we have only *futurum* and seek a transformed humanity on the basis of only present realities, then our hope would risk dissolving into despair. Our vision of the new future would stand over us like God's law, only judging and condemning us for our failure to achieve it. *Adventus,* in contrast, is gospel—good news. In it is the hope that people will be transformed with at least the help of God himself. God's future kingdom will cancel out past sins and reconstitute humanity at a quality of life that transcends present existence. The gospel of eschatology is that beyond judgment and death there is forgiveness and resurrection.

In this time of acute future consciousness, it is important that Christians share their vision of the eschatological kingdom of God with others. This means recognizing elements of that same vision which may appear in the thoughts and rhetoric of non-Christians of good will. This is God's law, providing us with a source of ultimate value and with direction for setting present priorities in decision-making. But Christian eschatology offers something more than what secular or humanistic futurology is able to do alone, namely, the gospel, the good news that we are not left alone in our failings but that we can rely upon divine power to finally bring world history to its consummate fulfillment.

2
MILLENNIALIST AND APOCALYPTIC PERSPECTIVES

When most people think of the futuristic thrust in Christianity they think of millennialism. This is a convenient mistake. It is a mistake because the futuristic thrust is central to Christian faith as a whole, whereas millennialism can easily be identified with sectarian and fringe points of view. It is convenient because by so identifying the future concern with the fringe, mainline denomination Christians can justify not facing up to their responsibilities.

Millennialism is only one expression of a much wider form of Christian thinking, namely, apocalypticism. I will argue that if we go beyond millennialism we will find in the apocalyptic view some valuable perspectives for constructing a viable Christian eschatology.

MILLENNIALISM

Millennialism certainly has its problems. First, its interpretation of the Bible is myopic. In its naive concern to protect the literal accuracy of Scriptural prophecy, it fails to recognize the hermeneutical value of viewing its favorite texts within the wider context of Biblical and other apocalyptic literature. Second, it presents us with such a super-individualized interpretation of Scripture that it functions to justify social irresponsibility. The millennialists seem to argue that because God will control the ultimate course of cosmic destiny we as individuals have no responsibility other than keeping ourselves clean and pure regardless of the evils mounting up around us. It seems that both those who believe in millennialism and those who do not, find this doctrine a comfort in their lethargy.

The term "millennialism" comes from the Latin *mille annum* meaning one thousand years, and harks back to the notorious passage in Revelation 20 where Satan is bound for that period. It is sometimes referred to as "chiliasm" from the term's counterpart in Greek, *chilia eta*. Millennialists or chiliasts focus their attention on such themes as the second coming of Christ or parousia, the tremendous struggle between the forces of good and evil that is expected to directly precede the parousia, the rapture, predictions about the place of the Jews in God's kingdom, the Last Judgment, the resurrection of the dead, and the final defeat of evil and renewal of all things at the establishment of God's everlasting kingdom. The key passage is Revelation 20:2–3:

> And he seized the dragon, that ancient serpent, who is
> the Devil and Satan, and bound him for a thousand
> years, and threw him into the pit, and shut it and sealed
> it over him, that he should deceive the nations no more,
> till the thousand years were ended. After that he must
> be loosed for a little while.

Millennialism falls into three basic schools: *post*millennialism, *pre*-millennialism and *a*millennialism. The various positions are determined by the point at which each school locates the second coming of Christ in relation to the 1000-year period, i. e., after, before, or during, respectively.

Postmillennialism, as its name suggests, asserts that Christ's parousia will occur *after* his 1000-year reign over the chained devil. The power over Satan during this period is not conceived as the personal reign of Christ so much as the reign of his church in society. The thousand years—and there are divergent views within this school regarding how literally or figuratively the 1000 years are to be understood—refer to the golden age of the church.

The period of the church is characterized as the time for the worldwide preaching of the gospel and the victory of faith over unfaith. It is a time when both Jews and Gentiles will be converted and come into the church. The golden era will be followed by a brief period of apostasy and then a dreadful conflict between Christian and evil forces. The conflict will be ended by the intervention of the heavenly champion, Christ. With the return of Christ will also come a general resurrection of the dead and the great white throne of judgment that separates the good from the evil for all eternity.

The postmillennial doctrine fits in well with the wider atmosphere of nineteenth-century liberalism in both church and Western culture. It was a period of optimism, and many Christians felt they were already in the millennium. Nineteenth-century Westerners believed in progress; they could see that world history was drawing humanity out of the dark ages of the primitive past and into the light of modern civilization.

People of the twentieth century cannot accept this naive optimism, however. Moral progress has stopped, if not reversed. Two world wars, the conversion of 5 million Jews not into Christians but into ashes, atomic warfare, and the hoarding of surplus food in the face of mass starvation—all perpetrated by the civilized "Christian" nations—all this removes any ground for belief that Christ now rules and that the devil is chained. Postmillennialism is dead; unless, of course, it interprets the twentieth century as the period of apostasy and the unchaining of the dreadful forces of evil.

The amillennials or nonmillennials are closer to this postmillennialist view than are the premillennialists. The nonmillennialist view is in concert with traditional Lutheran and Calvinistic understandings of Christian doctrine. Here Revelation 20 is interpreted figuratively. The one thousand years are thought to be symbolic of the present period of Christ's reign in the church. The chaining of the devil represents the power of the gospel to work victory in the heart of the believer, bringing him or her from unfaith to faith. It is the power of conversion and the daily conquering of sin. The present period of the church is the period between Christ's first advent in the manger on the first Christmas and the second advent still expected at the close of the age.

Neo-orthodox theology similarly recognizes the figurative nature of Revelation 20, if and when it takes this passage seriously at all. The second coming of Christ is his real presence in the proclamation of the gospel, referred to usually as the kerygma or Word of God. The first coming was a historical coming in the person of Jesus. The second coming, termed "eschatological," is the spiritual Christ in the Word as it is preached and responded to in faith. This proclaimed gospel has the power to change one's life, to free the individual from his or her own past neuroses, to remove past fears and anxieties, and to open up a bright future for a now revivified and wholesome personality.

Even though the Apocalypse of John speaks about the parousia and future kingdom of God in social and cosmic terms, for the Neo-orthodox it is really only a symbolic way of describing the working of God's Word in the individual at the existential level. Revelation's vision of the future really describes individual human existence before God in the present. Hence, we can say that orthodox or traditional nonmillennialists retain belief in an actual historical parousia in the future, whereas Neo-orthodox thinkers for the most part give this up in favor of a Christ already come back and living now in his Word. What both have in common is a rather figurative or symbolic approach to interpreting the relevant Scriptural passages.

Premillennialism is the most prominent and virulent of the three, and the most inclined to make literal application of what is said in John's Apocalypse. Its most vigorous advocates can be found in the Jehovah's Witnesses, Seventh Day Adventists, Mormons, and some conservative Evangelicals on the right wing of Protestantism. The premillennialists contend that Christ will come in the future to inaugurate the startling program that constitutes the thousand-year reign on earth.

The premillennialist sequence of events looks like this. At the inauguration of the millennial reign, Christ will return physically and set up his headquarters in Jerusalem. At this time the first general resurrection will occur; the righteous dead will be raised again to life and they will participate with Christ in his reign from Jerusalem. The now destroyed Temple will be rebuilt. There will be a mass conversion of Jews and Gentiles. Satan will be bound and civilization and nature will be free from his power. Peace and harmony will reign. Wolves will lie down with lambs, etc.

At the end of the millennium Satan will be loosed for a season (Rev. 20:7–10). Then the second resurrection will occur, wherein both the righteous and unrighteous will be raised. Everyone then will stand before the great white throne of God to be judged (Rev. 20:11–15). If your name is found written in the book of life you will receive eternal glory. If your name is not found in that book, you will be thrown along with Death and Hades into the lake of fire to be destroyed forever. What follows is the creation of a new heaven and a new earth and the establishment of an eternal kingdom of blessedness by God (Rev. 21).

The inauguration of the millennium will be preceded by a series of calamities known as the Great Tribulation, and many premillennialists hope to escape the Tribulation by being raptured. Based on 1 Thessalonians 4:17, "rapture" refers to the expectation that the saints will be catapulted into the air and taken to safety by Christ, thereby escaping the agonies of earth's Tribulation. A popular dash-sticker says: "If I'm Raptured, Take the Wheel!"; while a corresponding bumper-sticker reads: "In Case of Rapture, This Vehicle Will Self-Destruct."

Orthodox objections to premillennialism usually point out that it ends up with two second comings, two resurrections, and, implicitly, two judgments. Premillennialism is usually accompanied by claims that contemporary seer-like interpreters of the Bible have located in present world events precise fulfillments of Biblical promises. They claim the end is near and that it can be calculated sometimes to the day for those who can read the signs of the times. The orthodox denominations object, saying that if even God's son did not know (Mark 13:32) then it is somewhat presumptuous for a fresh high school graduate going door to door with an armful of tracts to claim such knowledge.

One brand of premillennialism is dispensationalism. It gets its name from the term "dispensation," defined as a period of time during which people are to be tested by their obedience to some specific revelation of the will of God. The *Scofield Reference Bible* rigorously divides the history of God's dealings with the human race into seven successive dispensations: innocence, conscience, civil government, promise, law, grace, and the kingdom. We stand at present between grace and the kingdom.

One of the most popular contemporary dispensationalists in the tradition of Cyrus Ingerson Scofield (d. 1921) and John Nelson

Darby (d. 1882) is Hal Lindsey. Lindsey's book *The Late Great Planet Earth* has sold about two million copies, and he has followed it with two other popular works *Satan Is Alive and Well on Planet Earth* and *There's a New World Coming.* With the help of freelance journalist C. C. Carlson, Lindsey is able to present quite a spicy rendering of the Biblical prophecies. With all the cute quips typical of Alka-Seltzer and Ex-Lax commercials, he renames the antichrist the "Future Fuehrer" and refers to the whore of Babylon in Revelation 17 as "Scarlet O'Harlot."

Lindsey engages in Biblical hopscotch—jumping from one part of the Bible to another without regard to context—in order to piece together a coherent vision of Biblical prophecy that can interpret the contemporary political and social scene.[1] He concentrates on the period of "Tribulation" and authoritatively argues that what we see going on in the world today is a sign that the end is near. In fact, all the Biblical predictions he can put his hands on are expected to achieve fulfillment within forty years of May 14, 1946, the date of the establishment of the state of Israel.[2]

Lindsey believes that modern Israel is the key to unlocking the mysteries of Biblical prophecy. Somehow he has determined that the period of Tribulation (Matt. 24:21) and the battle of Armageddon (Rev. 16:16) could not take place until the Jews had returned to their homeland. This return of the Jews, he says, was foretold in Ezekiel 37—38; therefore after this initiation the rest of the predicted events are about to follow like clockwork.

But Lindsey like others bent on making so-called "literal" interpretations of Scripture completely avoids analyzing the Bible in terms of its own historical context. In the case of Ezekiel 37—38, the prophet was living with his fellow Jews in exile in Babylon. The whole nation had been removed from its homeland by the notorious Babylonian king Nebuchadnezzar. Ezekiel was predicting that God would restore his people to their land. And he did so. Babylonian power waned a half-century later, and the Persians gained hegemony over the Middle East. The new emperor, Cyrus of Persia, sent the Jews home. Ezekiel's prophecy was fulfilled.

There is a sense, I suppose, in which we might say that Ezekiel's prophecy was fulfilled a second time following World War II. And if Ezekiel's prophecy is subject to multiple fulfillments, it would follow that Israel could conceivably lose its homeland once again only to return at a still later occasion. If Lindsey is going to disregard the importance of the first fulfillment in historical antiquity, then it is conceivable that the Tribulation will be tied not to 1946 but to some other future return of the Jews. A mere glance at the historical context of Ezekiel's writing puts Lindsey's literal interpretation on thin ice.

Undaunted by such considerations, Lindsey plunges on. The beast with seven heads and ten horns in Daniel 7 and Revelation 13 is really the European Common Market. He says the antichrist is about to set up a ten-nation European confederacy as a base from which he will attempt to unify the world under the aegis of evil. Between the publication of Lindsey's first and third books, Norway declined to join the European Common Market. The total participating nations were then nine, one short of ten. This too was dubbed part of God's plan, an action to prevent too rapid a consolidation.

According to Lindsey's calculus, Russia turns out to be Gog in Ezekiel 38:16, the invader from the north in Daniel 11:40 and Joel 2:20, and the rider of the red horse in Revelation 6:4. The National and World Council of Churches turn out to be the whore of Babylon, who will seduce us all into joining a one-world religious system. The NCC and WCC are apostate, Lindsey says, because they are divided by constant controversy over social and political issues instead of unified in the one gospel. Nevertheless, these *divided* bodies are somehow supposed to *unite* the world into a single apostate religion. And when Gog from the north, Russia, threatens war, in defense and out of fear of atheistic communism the one-world political system centered in the European beast will be driven into the arms of the harlot, the one-world religious system. The result will be an oppressive theocracy organized in an attempt to defeat God; or is it to defeat Russia? Is Gog really God? Who are the good guys and who are the bad guys, anyhow? Well, maybe they are all bad guys, because the good guys will be raptured before the battle begins.

The pre-Tribulation rapture will remove the righteous of God from the battle scene on earth, permitting them to escape the calamities. Using LSD jargon Lindsey calls it "the ultimate trip." He challenges each of his readers to climb on board.

> He is coming to meet all true believers in the air. Without benefit of science, space suits, or interplanetary rockets, there will be those who will be transported into a glorious place more beautiful, more awesome, than we can possibly comprehend. Earth and all its thrills, excitement, and pleasures will be nothing in contrast to this great event.
> It will be the living end. The ultimate trip. . . . The big question is, will you be here during this seven-year countdown? Will you be here during the time of the Tribulation when the Antichrist and the False Prophet are in charge for a time? Will you be here when the world is plagued by mankind's darkest days?[3]

This is pie-in-the-sky escapism, and literally in the sky. Apart from determining whether what Lindsey is saying is true or not, obviously we can see that the tone is one that says: get right with God now so you won't be destroyed when your neighbor is. The solution to the problem of evil in the world is to run away from it. If this world is going to hell then we should be buying tickets to go to heaven, to another world. I do not say that there is no precedent for this kind of message in the Bible; but I certainly believe the thrust of the New Testament is to have courage and take responsibility to *face* evil, not flee it. As God was incarnate in Christ because he refused to flee the forces of evil, so also are we promised that the Spirit will dwell in us to continually overcome the same forces. This does not make tribulation a picnic, but it helps to give us confidence and hope in the face of it.

Also, if we press the point too fiercely that the good guys will be taken up on the ultimate trip, we just might find ourselves on the wrong end of the wave good-bye. Recall, one essential ingredient in the gospel is the forgiveness of sins—our own sins! The absolutely unavoidable step that must be taken by a Christian coming to faith is the recognition that she or he is a sinner. Lindsey enjoys pointing out the sins of nearly everybody on this planet but himself. The antichrist is always somebody else, not me! The buck never stops at home. Jesus blistered his contemporaries for hypocrisy whenever they drew a line between good and evil people and then put themselves on the good side. The gospel challenges us to look first for the enemy of God not out there somewhere but in our own heart.

A Christian saint is always a forgiven sinner, and as such is a disciple of Christ in *this* world. God so loved this world that he sent his son to serve in it; his followers are similarly called. Any interpretation of the New Testament that directly or indirectly incites us to hate the world enough to want to leave it flies in the face of the purpose of God's act of redemption.

§

We might ask ourselves to what extent secular future consciousness can be productively interpreted from the millennialist perspective. The first thing to note is that at least in its premillennialist form it is simply out of tune with the secular. Scientific forecasts regarding ecological calamities or mass starvation are not seen as problems for human decision-making but rather as signs of supra-human cosmic forces hastening the predicted day of destruction. Furthermore, millennialism itself seems to generate such confusion and contradictions within its own camp that there is considerable doubt that it can genuinely reflect the central message of the Bible. It would be premature, then, to press millennialism to provide an adequate Christian hermeneutic for secular experience.

Millennialism is based upon only a fragment of the wider Biblical witness. In addition, it is only one of many approaches to the immediate context in which it originally appeared, namely, apocalyptic. Perhaps a brief look at apocalyptic in general will broaden the scope of our study and uncover additional resources for dealing with future consciousness.

APOCALYPTICISM

The book of Revelation is part of a wider tradition in literature that extends beyond the bounds of the New Testament, namely, apocalyptic literature. The term "apocalypse" is a Greek word meaning to "unveil" or "reveal," and in particular it has come to refer to revelations regarding the future. The Greek name for the last book of the Bible—left untranslated in Roman Catholic Bibles

—is the Apocalypse of John. The term calls to mind an audience in a theater waiting for the performance to begin. Suddenly, the curtain is drawn back, and there on the stage is the drama of the impending future. Apocalyptic literature is characterized by bizarre visions and wild symbolism, all enforcing the sense of drama as the future unfolds.

Along with the book of Revelation in the New Testament, the teachings of Jesus in Mark 13, Matthew 24—25 and Luke 21 are apocalyptic in character. But Jesus did not invent apocalyptic thinking; it was already present when Jesus appeared on the scene. In fact, what Jesus and the apostles taught was in large part interpreted and understood by their first-century followers in terms of the apocalyptic framework already familiar to them.

Thus, apocalyptic forms the background for the New Testament. The literature we have in mind is basically Jewish in origin, dating from about 200 B.C. to A.D. 100, and including such writings as Daniel, I and II Enoch, Jubilees, Sibylline Oracles, XII Esdras, and II and III Baruch. The millennium prophesied in Revelation 20 has its precedent in 2 Esdras 7:28ff., wherein the earthly rule of the Messiah is said to last four hundred years, following which the Messiah will die and the now dead will awake to face judgment. Other more general apocalyptic themes relevant to New Testament interpretation include contentions regarding the end of world history, the coming of the Son of Man, the Last Judgment, the resurrection of the dead, the destruction of the old and the creation of the new, the establishment of the eternal kingdom of God, etc. Three of these themes in particular will concern us in this book: the resurrection of the dead, the concept of temporal history, and the future kingdom of God.

In the apocalyptic verse Daniel 12:2 a future resurrection from death with judgment for both the good and the wicked first appears in the Bible: "And many of those who sleep in the dust of the earth shall awake, some to everlasting life, and some to shame and everlasting contempt." The historical context of the book of Daniel is important for understanding it. Many Biblical scholars believe that it was probably written after Alexander the Great had established Greek control over Palestine, and perhaps more precisely between

167 and 164 B.C., during the reign of Antiochus IV (Epiphanes). Great pressure was being put on the Jews to become integrated into the Greek civilization, and those Jews who resisted were severely punished. After appointing his own puppet Jewish high priest, Antiochus IV (Epiphanes) sacrificed a pig on the altar in the Temple at Jerusalem, and then compelled Jews to join the cult of Zeus. Many Jews who defied the order were put to death. The book of Daniel, anticipating as it does a future divine retribution, expresses the heartfelt protest of the people against political oppression and their inner anxiety over suffering.

The notion of God's judgment falling upon disobedient and wicked people had always been present in the Bible, but rather than being otherworldly it was first conceived as a judgment here on earth and during our lifetime. God and the people of Israel had made a covenant which was characterized by promise and law. God promised to free the Israelites from Egyptian oppression and deliver them to the promised land "flowing with milk and honey"; the people, on their side, were expected to keep the Ten Commandments. With the leadership of Moses and Joshua God fulfilled his promise. But once in the land the Hebrews decided to switch to worshiping the fertility gods of Canaanite Baalism, a violation of commandments one to three. In addition, an aristocratic class arose who used their newfound power "to oppress the fatherless and the widow," so that a situation of social injustice ensued, a violation of the last seven commandments. After repeated warnings from the prophets that went unheeded, God permitted the Assyrian armies to devastate the ten northern tribes of Israel in 721 B.C. The southern tribes failed to return to the covenant, so judgment was wrought when Nebuchadnezzar's armies captured Jerusalem and carried the Jews off to captivity in Babylonia in 587 B.C. Wicked disobedience to the covenant was met with justice, but it was a this-worldly sort of justice. The first Psalm declares: "Blessed is the man who walks not in the counsel of the wicked. . . . In all that he does, he prospers . . . but the way of the wicked will perish."

But the situation had changed by the time of Antiochus IV (Epiphanes). Now, it seemed, the wicked were prospering while those most faithful to God and his covenant were perishing. It was because of their loyal faith in God that people suffered from the persecution, even to the point of dying and losing all opportunity for God to make just compensation on earth. The question was raised: how can God be justified now that loyal and innocent people are suffering and being put to death? This is known as the theodicy problem: how can we reconcile God's goodness and omnipotence with the existence of evil in the world?

Dissatisfaction with present injustice led apocalyptic writers to look for a resolution of theodicy in the future beyond the grave. God is the creator of all things, with power over life and death, and he has certainly proven himself to be a God of promise and justice, so it must follow that his goodness will be vindicated beyond the grave. The faithful will not be forsaken in death. The history of the world thus becomes divided into two eons: the present evil age, alienated from God and characterized by injustice and suffering, and the future age in the kingdom of God's heaven, wherein the resurrected dead will live in harmony with the divine will and with each other. Heaven or paradise began to be described as a place "prepared for the righteous, who suffer offense in their lives and spite in their souls, and avert their eyes from injustice and make righteous judgement, to give bread to the hungering, to clothe the naked and cover them with a garment, to raise the fallen, and help the wronged, who walk before God's face and serve him alone." (II Enoch 9:1)

In Jesus' parable of the rich man and Lazarus (Luke 16:19–31) the situation beyond death reverses the situation on earth. The rich man, "clothed in purple and fine linen and who feasted sumptuously every day," had failed to share his wealth—given him by God's grace—with a poor man, Lazarus. Every Jewish landowner was really God's tenant (Lev. 25:23), and was thus expected to share the bounty of the land in the form of alms (Isa. 58:7). The rich man's failure to heed the sufferings of Lazarus, who was so enfeebled from lack of food that he could not even stop the street dogs from licking his sores, meant he would be subject to God's judgment. Lazarus is carried off to heaven, eternally liberated from oppression and suffering, while the rich and insensitive aristocrat is sent to Hades. The apocalyptic tenor of this parable reflects the wide dissatisfac-

tion with present injustices, but counting on God's already demonstrated integrity it promises a future salvation and vindication of
God's justice.

What has happened is that the previous this-worldly vision of the
future fulfillment of God's promises understood in the Old Testament
has been replaced with an otherworldly vision. "The earth, as it is,
has now come to be regarded as wholly unfit" for the establishment
of God's kingdom.[4] The present world must be replaced with a new
and transformed one; the present evil age must give way to a future
purified age. With the close of the present age, history will come
to an end. And with its end in sight, history can now be seen as a
whole, as a unity.

Apocalyptic thinks in terms of universal history. Everything that
happens finds its meaning only in terms of God's ultimate resolution
in the eschaton. This is basically a temporal view of reality, not a
spatial one. It does not locate the essence of things in their depth,
at some inner spiritual core, nor in an eternal sphere tangential to
our temporal sphere. Time and being are running a straight line from
the original creation and its fall into sin in the past, to judgment and
re-creation in the future. Apocalyptic takes the Old Testament view
that reality is essentially historical.

And the apocalyptic notion of history is distinctly deterministic
and pessimistic. Daniel says "what is determined shall be done."
(Dan. 11:36) There is an inevitability to history. Through travail and
persecution it will move unerringly toward its predetermined goal.

Apocalyptic writings frequently refer to heavenly tablets upon
which God has recorded the fixed order of historical events. On
these tablets is written "all the deeds of mankind, and of all the
children of the flesh that shall be upon the earth to the remotest
generations." (Jubilees 1:29) The Day of Judgment will come when
the fixed number of the elect has been achieved (2 Esdras 4:35–36;
11:44; 14:5). Not only is the ultimate end or goal determined, in
many cases the specific course of world events has been preor-
dained.

In addition to this divine determinism the present eon is filled
with great superhuman forces of evil over which individual people
have no control. God has abandoned this age to the scourge of

Satan and his demons. Humans stand virtually powerless before the terrors and calamities wrought by demonic forces. Overwhelmed and inundated by the fury of wickedness all around, one can only hope that God in his grace will rescue us as individuals and carry us through to the new eon. In itself the old eon is without meaning or purpose; our only goal is to escape from it.

What seems to have gotten the present eon off to a bad start in terms of God's cosmic plan is human selfishness. Selfishness is the sin that separates our age from God's; it lets loose the demonic powers of greed and strife that overwhelm us.

> The beginning of troubles in every case is a lack of understanding and greed.
> For there arises the striving after deceitful gold and silver. . . .
> It is the source of godlessness and the signpost to disorder,
> Cause of all wars, hateful enemy of peace,
> It makes the children hate their parents and the parents their children.
>
> [Sibylline Oracles VIII. 17ff.]

Apocalyptic is very pessimistic about this world. History is on a downward course that cannot be stopped. The seer of IV Esdras (7:116) cries "it would be better if the earth had never brought forth Adam." Pessimism leads to resignation; it ends in a nihilistic understanding of present existence. Such pessimism and nihilism destroy confidence and dampen enthusiasm. They lead to the renunciation of any responsibility on our part for the fate of this world's course.

Walter Schmithals goes so far as to identify apocalyptic pessimism with the disdain for the physical world in gnosticism. At one level, of course, these two movements seem quite different: gnosticism reflects the cyclical notion of time whereas apocalyptic presumes time to be linear (see chapter 5 below: "Time and History"). But at a deeper level, Schmithals points out, both are heavily dualistic.[5] Gnosticism draws a sharp line between the divine world of spirit and light over against the physical world of flesh and darkness. Spirit is good and flesh is evil. Salvation consists in receiving true en*light*enment or knowledge—*gnosis*—and then allowing the soul to escape from the body to enter spiritual heaven.

Apocalyptic is a temporal, not a spatial, dualism. The present evil age is just as repugnant to the apocalyptic mind as the world of flesh is to the gnostic. Salvation similarly consists in escape by the individual.

Schmithals also points out that such hopelessness does not represent the opinion of apocalyptic proper so much as it does that of the pessimism widespread in the environment. It is much more indicative of the negative view of the world held by those to whom apocalyptic was originally addressed.[6] There is optimism in apocalyptic as well—its optimism is its response to the widespread pessimism. A new age is coming.

We are challenged to decide whether we want to remain a part of the old eon and share in its destruction or to side with righteousness and pass through the purgatorial fires and be resurrected into the new.

This challenge to choose raises a question in the minds of modern interpreters of ancient apocalyptic: if history has been so rigidly determined in advance, then what is the role of human freedom in this scheme? If events have been predetermined, then are we really able to make free decisions of consequence? If this world has been abandoned by God, and if what we intend to do can accomplish nothing for the good, then what does it matter that we make decisions at all?

H. H. Rowley and D. S. Russell say that according to the apocalyptic view divine activity does not override or eliminate human freedom. This conflict is a much more modern concern. Apparently it was not a problem for the theologians of this period. Russell writes: "The clash of human freedom and divine control had not as yet become a conscious problem, so that these two apparently contradictory points of view could be expressed side by side without any intellectual difficulty."[7] The book of Jubilees, for example, can say that each person's path is set out and that the heavenly tablets already contain the record of one's judgment; at the same time it counsels individuals to take heed and not walk in the way of transgression lest judgment become written down against them (Jubilees 5:13; 41:24ff.). And the author of Psalms of Solomon 9:7 writes, "O God, our works are in our choice, yea, in the power of our own soul: to do either righteousness or iniquity in the works of our hands." And a non-apocalyptic Jewish thinker, Rabbi Akiba, said: "All is foreseen, but freedom of choice is given." (Pirkē Aboth 3:16)

The significance of human decision and action, then, is not dissolved by the apocalyptic vision of history. It does tend, however, to focus strongly on the individual rather than the community or the world as a whole. In the face of the coming judgment, in which God will separate the righteous from the unrighteous, it is the responsibility of each soul to choose its own fate. "Each one of them has prepared for his own soul torment to come, and again each one of them has chosen for himself glories to come." (II Baruch 54:15) The aim of our decisions is not to grab hold of the reigns of history as a whole and steer it in another direction. That direction has already been determined. Rather, we are enjoined to identify ourselves with that supra-historical or post-historical goal: the kingdom of God. It is assumed that God's kingdom wants *us,* not the world we will be leaving behind.

The projection of a future kingdom of God is the strong optimistic conclusion to the apocalyptic vision. It is its *raison d'être.* The term "kingdom," *basileia,* need not imply mere geographical hegemony. *Basileia tou Theou* can also be translated "reign of God." Wherever his reign is absolute, there his kingdom is in power. It can apply to the heart and will of the individual believer, or it can apply to society as a whole. For apocalyptic, the kingdom refers to God's eschatological rule within every human heart, all of society, and even nature.

It will be the final achievement of the messianic promise for peace on earth. There will be only one world. Only a divided world can pick sides to have a war. Only a divided world can fight over its wealth and seek to hoard its riches for some to the exclusion of others. But division will give way to unity. Capitalistic selfishness will be subordinated to communal sharing. In God's kingdom there will be equality.

> The earth is for all alike, and is not divided by walls
>   and boundaries,
> But it will bring forth much more fruit
> Entirely of itself: life will be shared by all in wealth
>   without overlords.

> Neither slaves nor masters will be there, neither lofty
>   nor lowly ones,
> Neither kings nor princes, and all are equal.
>
> [Sibylline Oracles II. 319ff.]

The energies of nature will cooperate with the energies of people to cultivate a productive economy and harmonious society.

> Health will be distilled in the dew, and sickness will be removed. And trouble and woe and laments will pass away from men, and joy will walk the whole earth, and no one will die before his time, and nothing untoward will suddenly happen. And trials and accusations and controversies and deeds of revenge and envy and jealousy and hatred and all such will fall under condemnation, and will be uprooted. . . . And in those days the harvesters will not grow weary and those who build will not falter in their work. For the labors will progress by themselves, together with those who work on them in much peace.
>
> [II Baruch 73:1–4; 74:1]

And in a New Testament rendering of this vision, the kingdom will in addition bring comfort to the saddened.

> They shall hunger no more, neither thirst any more;
>   the sun shall not strike them, nor any scorching heat.
> For the Lamb in the midst of the throne will be their shepherd,
>   and he will guide them to springs of living water;
> and God will wipe away every tear from their eyes.
>
> [Rev. 7:16–17]

Kingdoms are normally run by a system of laws. So are republics, democracies, oligarchies, dictatorships, and various other forms of government large and small. When the laws are just and when they are obeyed there is domestic tranquillity. Peace is disrupted to the extent that the law is broken.

God's will is expressed in his law. Through the Old Testament Torah God presented his law in human history, but he did not present it with an accompanying government bent on coercion to enforce it. External coercion has not been the divine method of enforcement. The prophets and Jesus remind us that external observance of God's law is superficial; it is our hearts that God desires. Jesus summed up the law as loving God and loving neighbor. Love is deeply personal. It comes from the inside, not the outside. Jeremiah prophesied that God will make a new covenant with his people; but this time his law will be written on our hearts. Then there will be no need for teachers to teach it or soldiers to enforce it (Jer. 31:31–34).

In a sense, we now have God's law but not his kingdom. He does not yet reign in our hearts. The fulfillment of the law is yet outstanding. We await the marriage of law and government—and paradoxically the withering away of both—in the eschatological consummation of God's purposes for world history.

§

Perhaps we should now ask if and to what extent the apocalyptic vision can be relevant to the twentieth-century outlook on the future. Is it strictly a conglomeration of fairy tale visions encapsulated in primitive mythical language, a projection of wish-dreams for victory by a mentality depressed by defeat? Or is it a vision that is sufficiently grounded in the truth to provide a real beacon for seeing our way through the fog of uncertainty that confronts us? Is the world view of apocalyptic outdated or can it still challenge the modern mind to deeper self-understanding?

In the chapters following, I will suggest that at least three features of apocalyptic offer a valuable hermeneutical vantage point from which we may interpret our contemporary experience with future consciousness. First, apocalyptic provides the horizon for interpreting the meaning of Jesus' Easter resurrection, a meaning that endures to the present period. Second, although there are problems with the apocalyptic notion of history, it was this notion that provided a formative influence upon our modern historical consciousness. Third, the vision of the eschatological kingdom of God provides an ontological foundation for a set of values and priorities which orient us as we make decisions regarding our own future.

Nevertheless, I am not advocating a wholesale adoption of the apocalyptic program. There are two features of the ancient apocalyptic world view that are out of step with both the Old and New

Testaments, features which if adopted by our present age would be detrimental to our cause. The first is its absolute and total pessimism regarding human history. This apocalyptic belief is founded on the notion that God has abandoned our present age in favor of the future. The present eon is completely profane, devoid of divine intervention. The devil is the only lord. It follows then that we need not take any responsibility for the course of human history. We might as well give up the struggle.

In contrast, the Old Testament for the most part anticipated an event of salvation within the framework of history, an event modeled after the great historical act of God in the Exodus, when he rescued his enslaved people from the Egyptians. For the ancient Hebrews, God does not live only in another place, such as heaven, or in another time, such as the future. God may do that, but he is always at work here and now as well.

Because God is active in human history, we are ethically responsible. History has meaning. For the Deuteronomic historian what human beings do is very meaningful. In the books beginning with Deuteronomy and running through 2 Kings, the drama revolves around what people do in response to the covenant God has made with them through Moses on Mt. Sinai. When the Hebrews obey the covenant and demonstrate loyalty to God, God remains faithful and blesses them. But when they forget the covenant by worshiping other deities or by fostering grave injustices, God raises up an enemy to punish them. When his people repent of their evil and call again upon God, he delivers them from their burdens and once again offers them blessings. The important point here is that present history is meaningful, because both God and people take responsibility for what happens.

The same is true for the New Testament. The Christian kerygma begins with Jesus' resurrection on Easter. Certainly the meaning of Easter is dependent upon the apocalyptic context in which it was interpreted, but the strict apocalyptic understanding became altered in the process. Because the apocalyptic vision of a future resurrection of the dead was held by Jesus' followers, they interpreted what occurred on Easter as the future breaking into the present. What was expected to occur at the advent of the new eon *beyond* history was occurring already *within* history in the person of Jesus. The apocalyptic notion that God has abandoned the present eon has been proved false. Present history has meaning because God himself has entered into it.

Because God cares for what happens in human history, those who respond to God's care do so with a sense of the value of this world to God. It is *this* world that "God so loved . . . that he sent his only begotten son," and it is *this* world that will undergo transformation and renewal after the model of Jesus' resurrection to "everlasting life " (John 3.16, KJV) Because God has a purpose for this world, those who love God will want to share responsibility for the course of human history.

Certainly our secular futurists presume that human history has at least some meaning and, more important, that we humans have genuine responsibility. It is obvious that *we* have made the present crisis what it is; now the futurists ask us to shoulder the responsibility for resolving it. Insofar as the apocalyptic vision abandons all hope for human history this side of the end of the world, the motive for shouldering any responsibility is removed. This is counterproductive, to say the least.

The second feature of the apocalyptic world view that seems out of step both with canonical Scripture and with contemporary futurism is its individualistic escapism. If present history has been abandoned by God, then the strategic thing for individuals to do is to so identify with righteousness that they will be saved while the world falls apart around them. If the whole world is going down the drain, I can save my own skin by getting right with God now. Let the world go to hell; I am going to heaven.

This radical individualism is new with apocalyptic. In the Old Testament, the fate of the individual was bound up with that of the nation. The conduct of the national community much more than individual choice determined one's destiny. The individual was always seen as part of a larger whole. Even the prophets, often very isolated individuals, devoted their careers to the good of the entire community and not to obtaining salvation strictly for themselves. The apocalyptic individual must, of course, be righteous in order to escape history and go to God's heaven. But what does it mean to be righteous? One interpretation sees righteousness consisting strictly of obedience to the first table of the law: worship, prayer, and personal loyalty to God. It is a kind of doing good to God while avoiding doing good to neighbor; it lacks genuine ethical concern for people. During the religious reform under King Josiah about 625 B.C., the prophet Jeremiah ridiculed this kind of unethical righteousness. He said that although the Jews were spending sufficient time worshiping God in the Temple they were allowing rampant injustice to go unimpeded in the society around. *True* righteousness includes service to one's neighbor.

Similarly, Jesus denounced hypocritical righteousness because it covered up an inner selfishness. The rich young ruler who approached Jesus asking how he could enter the kingdom of God was a righteous man. He had obeyed all the commandments. But when Jesus asked him to sell all he had and give it to the poor, he could not do it. This reveals that the rich young ruler had obeyed God's commandments for selfish reasons, namely, in order to make *himself* good. He had not done so out of love for God or love for other people. This is a case of righteousness without ethical concern. It is this kind of person—who uses even God's law for the selfish purpose of reserving a divine reward—that Jesus blisters with the name "hypocrite."

The genesis of our present global crisis might loosely be referred to as the desire on the part of individuals to obtain the goodies of the planet at the expense of the rest of the world community. Individual people and individual interest groups seek their salvation not by identifying themselves with God's righteousness so that they might obtain eternal life beyond history. Rather, after taking a disproportionate share of the world's goodies, they "discount the future," i. e., they hope that the impending crisis will blow on past leaving them unruffled. It is a game of pretend, wherein the future judgment is thought to be either so far off as to be irrelevant to the present or else, if it does come, it will hurt the other guy and not me because I am "energy independent." This is certainly a cruder form of selfishness than that which we find in apocalyptic. Nevertheless, selfishness is the root problem regardless of its form.

For the weak, the oppressed, for those who are so overwhelmed by external forces of oppression and destruction that they have no control whatsoever over their destinies, the apocalyptic message of individual salvation comes as good news. In this case it is valid and important; it is not merely selfish escapism. It provides hope and courage, and even meaning in a fragmentary way. However, for those of us who share responsibility for the course of local or world events, apocalyptic escapism for the individual can serve to justify our most ungodly inclinations toward selfishness and toward shedding that responsibility.

3
CHRIST:
THE FUTURE MADE PRESENT

The New Testament sees in Jesus Christ the fulfillment of much that apocalyptic had been hoping for. The most obvious correlation is that of Jesus with the Son of Man or heavenly Messiah expected to usher in the new eon. Jesus stated repeatedly to his listeners, "the kingdom of God is in your midst." Most often this is interpreted to mean that Jesus himself was in their midst and in him God reigned completely. Jesus Christ was the embodiment of the new covenant promised by Jeremiah; he was the fulfillment of God's law in his own life. The kingdom of God had fully arrived, not for all of society or all of the cosmos, but in the person of Jesus. Christ is the future made present.

One day John the Baptist sent two of his disciples to Jesus to ask, " 'Are you he who is to come, or shall we look for another?' " Jesus responded by saying, " 'Go and tell John what you have seen and heard: the blind receive their sight, the lame walk, lepers are cleansed, and the deaf hear, the dead are raised up, the poor have good news preached to them.' " (Luke 7:19, 22)

The future kingdom of God promises that "health will be distilled in the dew, and sickness will be removed"; in the ministry of Jesus we find healing in his very touch. The future kingdom promises to dissolve social rank and remove master-slave divisions; Jesus' disciples included the outcast publicans and sinners even though he ate lunch with prestigious Pharisees such as Nicodemus. The future kingdom promises that "they shall hunger no more"; Jesus gave a sign by feeding four or five thousand people with five loaves and two fish. The future kingdom promises us a society in which God's law will be written on the hearts of its citizens; in the person of Jesus we can see God's incarnate love so totally that the unselfish lover was himself sacrificed to the present eon for expressing it.

In his person and in his teachings Jesus anticipated the future. The Lord's Prayer as transmitted to us by Matthew 6:9–13 and Luke 11:2–4 asks for God's kingdom to come. Following this—directly in the Lukan version but with an added petition in Matthew—it commonly reads: "Give us this day our daily bread." But the renowned New Testament scholar Joachim Jeremias suggests that a more accurate rendering would be: "Our bread for tomorrow, give us today."[1] He argues that the Greek for "daily bread," *artos epiousious,* is not a precise translation of what was most probably the original Aramaic, *mahar,* which means "tomorrow." Citing a reference in the writings of Jerome (circa A.D. 342–420), Jeremias describes this as an eschatologically oriented petition. In Judaism during this period, *mahar,* "tomorrow," meant not only the next day but also the great tomorrow, the final consummation. The "bread for tomorrow" meant not only daily sustenance but also the bread of life, "heavenly manna."

The petition as it is usually recited, then, does not preclude the request for "daily bread." But as originally intended it does ask more. It is another form of asking that "thy will be done" here and now as it is promised to be done in the future heaven. It asks that amid the secularity and evil of everyday life the powers and gifts of God's coming age might be actively at work.

With bread in mind, we might note how frequently Jesus' parables compare the kingdom of God with a great meal, often a wedding banquet: the wedding guests (Mark 2:19), the great supper (Luke 14:15–24, originally Q), the marriage feast and wedding garment (Matt. 22:1–13), the ten virgins (Matt. 25:1–13), and the places at table (Luke 14:7–11). He paints the picture of a grand eschatological feast to which we are issued an invitation; it is the Messianic Banquet. In the kingdom of heaven we will dine with God.

A prelude to this eschatological banquet took place during the Passover meal on the Thursday of Passion Week. After blessing the food Jesus took the bread "and broke it, and gave it to the disciples, and said, 'Take, eat; this is my body.' " Then, after identifying the wine with his blood, he declared: " 'I tell you I shall not drink again of this fruit of the vine until that day when I drink it new with you in my Father's kingdom.' " (Matt. 26:26, 29) Subsequently, to drink the wine and eat the bread of life during the sacrament of the altar is to get a foretaste of the consummation; it is to commune with the future fulfillment of all things. Christ is the future bread made present and mystically re-presented each time the sacrament is celebrated. He is tomorrow's bread given us today.

THE RESURRECTION

The most significant manifestation of the future kingdom of God in Jesus, however, is the Easter resurrection. The apocalyptic vision of an eschatological resurrection of the dead was confirmed by God in the experience of Jesus. The apocalyptic hope is not merely a projected wish-dream; it now has divine confirmation. This makes Biblical eschatology something serious to be reckoned with as the church confronts contemporary future consciousness. It is the foundation for hope even today.

Jesus' resurrection did not just suddenly appear on the stage of history. Nor is it simply the imaginative expression of subjective human hope to transcend the bounds of mortal existence. Rather, it gains its original interpretation and significance in the context of the Old Testament and the apocalyptic expectation.

For the most part, the Old Testament had no notion of individual immortality. The destiny of the individual was inextricably tied to that of the nation. God's promise seemed to have been given for the people as a whole. The kingdom of God was expected to occur on earth; and individuals looking forward to its advent took comfort in thinking that, though they themselves might not live to see it, they could be thankful that their descendants would receive its blessings.

The dead went to Sheol. Going to Sheol did not represent dropping off the scale of being entirely, however. The most primitive stage in the development of Old Testament eschatology allowed some influences from beyond the essential Hebrew tradition. One of these was a modest form of ancestor worship, the *teraphim*.[2] Sheol emerges as a kind of family or tribal grave, a dark shadowy extra-mortal existence from which some influence over future generations could be exerted, at least to the extent of demanding homage and sometimes sacrifice. In due course the conception of Sheol was expanded beyond the clan to embrace the departed of all nations, and thus it became conceived as the final abode for all humans.

Somewhere between the writing of second Isaiah (Isa. 40—55) and the Hellenizing pressures of Antiochus Epiphanes, there grew up an idea of resurrection from the dead. In the Daniel 12:2*a* passage cited in chapter 2, wherein those who "sleep in the dust of the earth shall awake," the term "dust" is associated with death and surely refers to Sheol.

Such resurrection was understood by analogy with awakening from sleep. The author of II Baruch 30:1 writes, "Then all those will arise who have gone to sleep hoping in him [the Messiah]." Ethiopian [i. e., I] Enoch 92:3 and 2 Esdras present us with a similar picture. It is not unusual for the Old Testament to use "to sleep" *(yashen)* to describe death (Jer. 51:39; Job 3:13; 14:12). "To awaken" *(quts),* then, would be a natural way to describe the revivification of the dead; and this term does appear in 2 Kings 4:31 to describe a dead child who " 'has not awakened.' "

The tradition that reaches into the New Testament is that of a metaphor with an implicit comparison between the destiny of the dead and rising from sleep. It is applied both to Jesus on Easter and to his followers at the advent of the consummate kingdom of God. Paul refers to the resurrected Jesus as "the first fruits of those who have fallen asleep." (1 Cor. 15:20)

It might at first appear that the analogy of sleeping and waking, when applied to dying and rising, would lead us to some notion of the revivification of the corpse, i. e., a return to life just as it had been lived previously. In the New Testament context, however, this image is an oversimplification. There are instances of corpses returning to life in the Biblical literature that are not equated with "resurrection from the dead" as applied either to Jesus on Easter or to the faithful at the end of our historical age. For example, the son of the widow at Nain (Luke 7:11–17), Lazarus (John 11:38–44), and the daughter of Jairus (Mark 5:21–43) were raised from the dead temporarily but, presumably, would still have to die again as a matter of normal course.

There is an element in our understanding of Jesus' resurrection which distinguishes it from these other three accounts and which necessitates metaphorical description. Jesus did not rise only to die again. The Biblical claim is that he rose for all eternity; nobody else has done that. The resurrection of Jesus was not simply the revivification of his corpse; it was the prolepsis. "Prolepsis" means the anticipation of a future reality in a concrete pre-actualization of it. The Easter resurrection was for him the arrival—and for us the promise—of the eschatological future itself.

In the Gospel accounts of the post-resurrection appearances, those to whom Jesus appears do not simply report "we have seen Jesus." Rather, they say "we have seen *the Lord.*"(John 20:18, 25; 21:7; Luke 24:34, emphasis added) Lazarus, Jairus's daughter, and the widow's son were seen alive after their deaths, but none were called "Lord." Raymond Brown argues that because "Lord" is a Christological evaluation of Jesus, the Gospel writers are saying that through the resurrection Jesus has been elevated to the position of Lordship in the kingdom of God. The texts report not only the *sight* of Jesus' resurrected body but also the *insight* into his eschatological significance.[3]

We find more detail in 1 Corinthians 15, where Paul contends that resurrection means new life to a new body and not simply the return of life into a dead but not yet decayed fleshly body. Paul seems to be rejecting the crassly material conception held by some apocalypticists, whereby the risen body would resume all the qualities characteristic of life this side of the grave. II Baruch 50:2, for example, says that when the earth restores the dead "it shall make no change in their form; but as it has received them, so it shall restore them." Over against this, Paul presents the resurrected body as different from the present—not a fleshly body but a "spiritual body." Resurrection involves transformation. The present earthly body may be sown perishable, dishonored, weak, and physical, but it is raised imperishable, in glory, in power, and spiritual (1 Cor. 15:42–44).

Of course, Paul in 1 Corinthians 15 is not speaking of Jesus' resurrection in particular, but about that expected by all waiting Christians. But it seems he must have had the same mental image of the resurrection of Jesus because he parallels Jesus' Easter experience with that yet awaiting the Christian believers at the end of the present eon (1 Cor. 15:15–19). What is important here is to note that the description of Jesus after Easter is not presented in terms applicable to a resuscitated corpse. Rather, it applies only to the kind of permanently resurrected body which is the apocalyptic expectation at the advent of God's kingdom.

CAN WE STILL BELIEVE IN EASTER?

It is difficult for us in the age of modern science and technology to accept an ancient claim that a man rose from the dead. Scoffers disregard the Christian faith as a religion founded on myths and fairy tales carried over into the modern world from a prescientific era. Contemporary civilization is supposedly hard-nosed about miracles; we now know there are no such things. There is only mother nature, and she rules with invincible laws. It is contrary to the laws of nature for the dead to return to life: therefore, Jesus remained dead and so will we.

Even so, the claim that "Jesus is risen" is so central to the Christian faith that faith cannot jettison it and still be called "Christian." Paul said, "if Christ has not been raised, then our preaching is in vain and your faith is in vain." (1 Cor. 15:14) The Easter resurrection after the Good Friday crucifixion is the kernel of the New Testament gospel, the basic content of the Apostles' and Nicene Creeds, the theme of countless church hymns, and the core of all evangelical theology. Consequently, these are difficult times for a person who wishes to be both intellectually honest and still affirm faith in Jesus Christ. Can it be done? I believe it can.

The problem is that the claim for Jesus' resurrection is a historical claim, and the study of history is the domain of secular or scientific historians for whom it is impossible to demonstrate that Jesus or anybody else ever rose from the dead. If it cannot be demonstrated by the methods of historical research that Easter actually occurred, then many fear that the historical grounding for Christian belief would be undercut.

It is because of this fear that many defenders of Christian faith in our century have radically reinterpreted what was traditionally meant by the New Testament claim, "he is risen." Some Existentialist and Neo-orthodox thinkers began applying the notion of the Easter event less to Jesus and more to his followers. Easter did not occur to Jesus; it happened to his disciples. Easter refers to the *rise of faith* in the living Christ which occurred in the first Christian community. The faith of this community can be safely documented historically; hence, the ground of Christian faith is preserved by faith itself.

Furthermore, the Easter resurrection is not limited to one time and place. It happens today, or whenever the gospel is proclaimed and a hearer responds to it by coming to faith. Willi Marxsen writes, "Jesus is dead. But *his* offer has not thereby lost its validity. That fact was experienced at the time and it can equally well be experienced today."[4]

Probably the most prominent exponent of this interpretation is Rudolf Bultmann. Bultmann believes in the resurrection as a "wonder," but it is an event that happens to the Christian believer in the moment of faith; it did not happen to the person of Jesus on Easter. "Resurrection" refers to the rising of faith and the sense of new life subjectively felt by the Christian community. It does not refer to an objective event in the history of Jesus.

In an interview that acquired the title "Is Jesus Resurrected like Goethe?" Bultmann affirms that Jesus' body remained in the tomb on Easter. His aim is not, of course, to present a case for the assertion that Jesus remained dead. He wishes rather to emphasize the importance of Christ living in present faith. Bultmann contends he is theologically neutral regarding questions as to the truth of the reports that Jesus rose. "As a matter of fact," he said, "the Easter faith has no interest in the historical question."[5]

The reason for this complete separation between what can be affirmed theologically and what can be determined through historical research is the present total acceptance of nature as a closed system. We believe nature to be a self-contained nexus governed by mechanical law. There are no miracles. Bultmann says that a person who uses the radio in the twentieth century cannot understand the meaning of the resurrection as long as it is tied to an outdated first-century mythological picture of the cosmos. Consequently, an intellectually respectable historical method must presuppose "that history is a unity in the sense of a closed continuum of effects in which individual events are connected by the succession of cause and effect."[6] With this presupposition, then, we must conclude that Jesus did not rise, because such an event would violate the cause-effect nexus determined by the laws of nature. It is just this unflinching dogma regarding the nature of nature that produces Bultmann's conclusion that the resurrection did not in fact occur as a historical event.

Note carefully just what it is about historical research that prevents it from concluding that Jesus in fact rose from the dead: it is the assumption that no one rises from the dead. But such an assumption is not part of the research itself.

The central element of scientific historiography involved here is the principle of analogy. In investigating a past event, the principle of analogy says that a comparison with what is already known provides a touchstone for evaluating the probability that the reported event actually occurred and for establishing its specific contours. Negatively put, if during historical investigation we are confronted with what the historian Marc Bloch terms "an overly-pronounced deviation" from what is analogous to our own experience, then the gaining of historical knowledge becomes *ipso facto* impossible.[7]

The philosopher David Hume relied upon the analogy principle in his critique of miracles. He said that because we have observed the apparent uniformity and universality of the laws of nature which are common to our daily experience, the laws of nature become the model for comparison. The historical events recorded in the New Testament are judged as possible if they are analogous to our understanding of events today. But it is here that Hume had trouble with the miracles. He defined a miracle as "a transgression of a law of nature by a particular volition of the Deity."[8] Thus, our common experience of the laws of nature to which such events must be found analogous weighs against the historical credibility of the miracle accounts. Because miracles do not conform to the laws of nature, we must only conclude that there are no such things as miracles. Of course, his very definition of miracle as that which breaks a law of nature led him into a circular argument which begs the question.

Ernst Troeltsch represents the same view, perhaps more developed. According to Troeltsch, the principle of analogy requires that there be a fundamental homogeneity or ontological sameness to all historical events. None violate the laws of nature, so all the historian need do is learn the laws of nature from the scientist in the laboratory next door before embarking upon the study of history. Since the nineteenth century, historical study has been swallowed up by a seventeenth-century theory of nature.

By subsuming history under the category of the study of nature, historians may not have taken with sufficient seriousness the character of their subject matter. Historians investigate individual or particular events for their own sake, whereas natural scientists seek to develop general or universal laws that apply to all events. The events of history are unique and unrepeatable, whereas the laws of nature can be exemplified time and again in repeated experiments. History records the decision and actions of humans with free will, whereas science looks for just those consistent patterns which are independent of human volition.

Interestingly, many leading scientists of the twentieth century have been willing to give up much of their previous belief in such things as the invincible laws of nature. Investigations into subatomic physics have led many researchers to disavow a static system of fixed laws and to rely more upon principles of probability. The world is in process and changing, and nature is constituted by a succession of unique and unrepeatable events in much the same way history is. Therefore, *every* event is unique; so a unique event such as the resurrection is certainly possible. Such theorizing remains the coffee-klatsch conversation of the inner circles of academic science, however, while the public school system still promulgates the more simplistic Newtonian view with its laws of nature that never go on a holiday. Consequently, it is ironic that the nonscientific public is much more disposed than is the sophisticated scientist to see the wide rift between natural law and the Christian claim that Jesus' resurrection was a unique event.

As a methodological principle for doing historical research, analogy has an essential and irreplaceable role. It simply means that something difficult to understand, something comparatively opaque, is to be conceived by the investigator in terms of what *is* understood. The objection we raise here is toward the negative use of analogy, which can be contrasted with the positive use. According to the positive use, if a reported event has an analogy with another actual event available to the inquiring historians' experience, then they judge that it is *possible* that the event did take place. Further evidence will be needed, of course, to determine if it is *probable* that it took place. For example, the positive use of analogy permits us to affirm that it is at least possible that Jesus was in fact crucified in the way that it is reported by the New Testament. The historian can compare this alleged event with reports of other crucifixions and similar forms of execution both past and present. The phenomenon of death is also subject to the experience of the historian. Consequently, Jesus' death is possible because positive analogies can be drawn between Jesus' death and other deaths.

The negative use of analogy reverses the direction: if there are no other events in the historian's experience which are analogous to the event under investigation, then it is believed that the alleged event could not have happened. It is not historical, i. e. factual. The central objection to the claim that Jesus rose from the dead rests upon this negative use of analogy. The implied argument takes the following form: because the inquiring historian has no other experience of a person rising from the dead, it follows that Jesus also did not rise from the dead. When historians turn to examine the New Testament reports, then, assuming that Jesus did not rise from the dead, they feel they must find some other factor which can explain those New Testament reports. The negative use of analogy necessarily presupposes the world view in which no one rises from the dead and that every event must conform to it. Negative analogy functions like a prejudice in the sense that it judges in advance, thereby forbidding any new event to change the historian's view of the natural world. If historical method can ever serve a theological analysis of Jesus' resurrection, it will have to be purged of this constricting tendency.

In seeking to find the best explanation for the New Testament reports, we must be *open* to the possibility that Jesus in fact did rise from the dead. An appeal to positive analogy alone does not discredit this possibility. What could we use for a positive analogy with Jesus' resurrection? Myths are part and parcel of the working historian's experience. But a critical examination of the New Testament does not reveal that the reports of Jesus' resurrection significantly correspond to myth. Jesus' resurrection was historical, not mythic.

There were myths of dying and rising divinities in the ancient world; however, they differ considerably from the New Testament metaphor we are concerned with here. In Greek mythology, Adonis was gored to death by a wounded boar, and where his saddened lover, Aphrodite, dropped his blood upon the ground crimson flowers would spring up fresh each year. The worship of Attis in ancient Rome recalled this god's death, following which, according to some stories, he was believed to have been changed into a pine tree, and according to other tales violets sprang up where his blood had been spilled. The Egyptian god Osiris was thought to die each year, and his buried corpse radiated life through the annual growth of vegetation.

Such myths obviously reflect—among other things—the seasons of the year and the argicultural cycle. They are repetitious and general in their structure. They do not present a single historical event as the referent to the phrase "resurrection from the dead." It would be unfair to drop the events of Jesus' career into this general barrel of dying and rising divinities without first doing justice to its specific historical context, i. e., the Old Testament and the Jewish apocalyptic tradition. This is what we have been attempting to do. The significant positive analogue to Jesus' experience is the expectation of a future resurrection—compared to rising from sleep —native to apocalyptic. This is how the early Christian church understood it. An open-minded examination will reveal that it is a viable way for us to understand it as well.

If the historian employs only positive analogy, he or she cannot in all honesty determine that Jesus did not rise from the tomb. Historical study must concern itself only with an investigation of the evidence, a critical assessment of the reliability of the witnesses or sources, and an open-minded attempt to draw a conclusion as to the most probable explanation for the experiences reported in the New Testament.

One of the first texts to be considered in such an examination is 1 Corinthians 15. Paul opens this chapter with a report of witnesses to the risen Jesus in much the style that a modern historian or journalist might employ. Paul reports that Jesus appeared to Cephas (Peter), the twelve, then to "more than five hundred" people, some of whom were still alive at the time of writing. Paul here is employing the kind of proof commonly used in the legal proceedings of his day. Herodotus and other Greek historians offered similar kinds of proofs. His evidence gathering consisted primarily in the interrogation of witnesses, and many of those Paul lists could still have been reinterrogated by anyone wishing to double-check his report.

Paul's authority is quite credible because he was close to the events themselves. The first epistle to the Corinthians was most probably written in A.D. 56 or 57. But the experiences of which he speaks occurred much earlier. If we were to date Jesus' death in the year 30, the conversion of Paul in the year 33, and then note that according to Galatians 1:18 Paul went to Jerusalem three years after his conversion, that would put him on the scene six years following the events. In Jerusalem he certainly spoke with Peter, the apostles, and other witnesses about the appearances to them of the risen Jesus. Jesus Christ in person had appeared also to Paul (Acts 9; 22; 26; Gal. 1), and it would seem natural for them to swap stories of their respective experiences. Thus, Paul had a firsthand knowledge of events which the Gospel accounts, generally thought to have been written later, did not have.

The four Gospels present reports of Jesus appearing to women at the tomb, to Peter, to the eleven disciples, to two followers at Emmaus, to doubting Thomas, etc. There are no reports of witnesses who claim to have seen the actual resurrection act itself, but only those who saw Jesus after he had risen. Although the oral traditions may date considerably earlier, the written records of the Gospels date in the last third of the first century and probably underwent more theological redaction based upon the then current situation of the church.

The Gospels also report that the tomb was empty on Easter, something Paul nowhere mentions specifically. However, we can expect that Paul counted on the emptiness of the tomb. Even the Jewish community at Jerusalem—the center of Christian activity in those first decades of the church's life—acknowledged that Jesus did not remain in the grave. It is difficult to imagine how Jesus' disciples could continue to proclaim his resurrection if their opponents could constantly point to the tomb where his corpse lay. Without reliable testimony to the emptiness of Jesus' grave, the early Christian community could not have survived in Jerusalem. And it more than survived; it grew.

It is now generally agreed that the bulk of the resurrection appearances took place in Galilee, whereas the discovery of the empty tomb naturally took place in Jerusalem. Historical critics identify the reports of appearance to the disciples and the empty tomb accounts as separate traditions. Perhaps the disciples left Jerusalem to return home shortly after the Good Friday execution; their journey to Jerusalem had resulted in such a catastrophic experience. They were disappointed and discouraged. But in Galilee the risen Christ appeared to them. Later, when they returned again to Jerusalem, they were met with others who reported how the tomb was found empty. It is very likely that the appearances and the discovery of the empty grave happened independently of each other and became connected only in later stages of the tradition. If this is the case, then we have a weighty reason for concluding that the Easter events were not the imaginative products of disturbed people but rather unique and real happenings. Wolfhart Pannenberg argues:

> If the appearance tradition and the grave tradition came into existence independently, then by their mutually complementing each other they let the assertion of the reality of Jesus' resurrection . . . appear as historically very probable, and that always means in historical inquiry that it is to be presupposed until contrary evidence appears.[9]

Of course, we must acknowledge that in some sense historical inquiry could not remain strictly secular when it offers up the conclusion that Jesus most probably rose from the dead on Easter. This is because the meaning of Easter and the fact of Easter are so closely tied together. Witnesses to the risen Jesus never claim merely that they saw a dead body returned to life; they claim they saw the "Lord." Jesus' resurrection is understood within its apocalyptic context, and that means Jesus has become the Christ, the Messiah, the right hand of God himself. Affirming that Jesus rose on Easter is simultaneously affirming that he is the Son of God. There must be a historical-factual ground for the Easter affirmation, to be sure, but this affirmation extends itself beyond the bounds of what is normally considered historical research and into the arena of faith. But faith does not believe only in itself; it affirms that God has acted decisively in human history.

In a sense, we need not contend that the Easter resurrection was a miracle. To do so may inadvertently endorse the view that natural law is definitive of reality, and it is this view that presented us with the problem in the first place. It is not important to Christian faith whether or not Jesus broke or did not break a law of nature on Easter. What is important is that in this event God's eschatological future became present and that the hopes of humanity for a new and better world have received divine confirmation.

LIVING THE FUTURE RESURRECTION NOW

The Easter of long ago is important to us today because it is determinative of our own future; what happened to Jesus is the proleptic anticipation of what will happen to us at the end of history. This event has meaning for us because our own destinies are tied to it. With the resurrection of Jesus, what for all other people is still to come has been realized. Therefore, faith in Jesus Christ gives us a ground for hope in a future beyond death, beyond the constrictions of a world fraught with hatred and innocent suffering. This hope for the future can change our relationship to the present.

This hope can provide meaning for us in the face of the challenge to commit ourselves to the cause of right even when the forces of wrong seem so overwhelming. Our awareness of the proliferation of nuclear dangers, of the hoarding of food in North America while a half billion go hungry in Africa and Asia, of our own technostructure which serves to block the poorer peoples of the world from obtaining a significant advance in their standard of living, and of the crude hedonism which has engulfed our culture through TV advertising and Hollywood sex—all this functions to deaden our consciences and narcotize our enthusiasm with a poison of failure. The problem is too big. And to row against the stream usually means ostracism, time in jail, or even an assassin's bullet. It seems that ethical courage is in need of vindication.

In the apocalyptic vision, resurrection first appears as a vindication of righteousness.[10] The book of Daniel among others reflects the historical backdrop of oppression and persecution. Resurrection functions as a divine confirmation of one's loyalty to God even when suffering unjustly at the hands of evil oppressors. And the Testament of Judah states: ''. . . those who died in grief will rise. . . . And those who die on account of the Lord will awake.'' (25:4a, c)

Similarly, the Easter resurrection is God's confirmation of Jesus' earthly life and ministry. As the Jews held fast to their pious loyalty to the Torah and as a result suffered under the pogrom of Antiochus, so also Jesus incarnated in himself the fullness of God's will and died for the Lord's sake. The resurrection signifies that he has already passed through the final judgment and been vindicated by God for his righteousness.

This calls to mind again the theodicy question. Originally coined by the philosopher Leibniz, the term ''theodicy'' comes from the Greek words *theos* (God) and *dike* (justice), and it literally means ''justification of God.'' Sometimes the question is asked this way: if God is supposed to be both all-powerful and all-loving, then why does he permit the evils of Vietnam and Auschwitz? If God is omnipotent, then he must justify himself as to why there is evil in the world. One way to resolve the dilemma—taken by theologians like Schubert Ogden—is to affirm the all-lovingness of the divine but admit that God is something less than all-powerful. The reverse is a second choice and equally logical, namely, that God is all-powerful and therefore the author of evil. The concept of God's wrath in meting out punishment to the Israelites in the Old Testament would tend to shift the weight toward the side of omnipotence. And then when evil befalls you for no apparent reason, the natural response would be that of Job's matter-of-fact wife: " 'Curse God, and die.' " (Job 2:9) A third approach is to leave the matter in the realm of "divine mystery," preventing a human assault on God's integrity. The great preacher Paul Scherer writes, "There are answers we have to live out, not spell out. No theodicy is possible. One cannot justify the ways of God to men."[11]

The German theologian of hope Jürgen Moltmann argues that the New Testament resolves the problem of theodicy in the cross and resurrection of Jesus Christ. God does not watch the suffering and dying of the crucified one from afar, sitting in his heaven, unconcerned with the events of human passion. "In Jesus' sacrifice is found the sacrifice of God himself. In Jesus' suffering God suffers; in his death, God himself tastes of damnation and death."[12] In the disturbing play *The Sign of Jonah* the actors search for someone they can blame for the evils of World War II. But the atrocities are so horrendous, the only person whose shoulders are big enough to bear the guilt is God himself. The court rules and God is sentenced. The punishment: God must become a man and suffer and die as we have. Of course, this has already been done. In his suffering, God ceases to be the defendant in the question of theodicy.

But not only is God's lovingness affirmed in the sufferings of Good Friday; his omnipotent justice is confirmed in the Easter resurrection. In his innocence and faithfulness Jesus was crucified. But God, in raising Jesus from the dead, confirmed that righteousness would finally be vindicated. God does have power over death and the power to make a new future which will resolve and heal all the injustices of the present. Moltmann writes, "Jesus' resurrection is the answer to the cry of the forsaken and the glorious beginning of the resolution to the question of theodicy in the world."[13] Jesus' crucifixion stands as a symbol of God's continual sharing in the sufferings and injustices of our present world; Jesus' Easter resurrection stands as a promise to those who are dissatisfied with the present eon that God himself is preparing a new future in his kingdom.

In contrast to the strict apocalyptic vision that recommends that we simply wait for the future resurrection of the dead, the Easter faith says that that future has already begun. The new eon has broken into the old. Therefore, to be at one with the new world in Christ gives us peace of mind as we face death to the old one. To tie ourselves to Easter gives us courage to know that our strivings for righteousness are not in vain. They are in tune with the ultimate destiny of the entire creation. In Christ God has promised vindication to those who seek to make his future kingdom a present reality. Hope based on this promise gives us the power to live resurrected lives now.

Without a hope of this sort all we have to look forward to is death and the ultimate obscurity of all our strivings. We begin to discount the future, i. e., we begin to concentrate on the present. Our more extravagant goals and ideals are trimmed and shaved to conform to the realities of the immediate situation. And the "eat, drink, and be merry for tomorrow we may die" syndrome overtakes us. Soon, selfishness becomes justified.

But hope for God's new world to come liberates us from strictly self-centered and present-oriented thinking. If our own ultimate destiny is in God's hands, then we alone are not the captains of our own souls. If we can trust that God's justice will be vindicated, and if we can trust the gospel message that by his grace we are justified, then we are free from the need to cram our present full with all the ephemeral gadgets and treats offered by a decaying technological civilization. And if we are *free from* ourselves we are *free for* loving others.

The future has already appeared proleptically in Jesus Christ. What was his destiny is now our destiny. But we need not simply sit on our hands waiting for the future to arrive. The future has the power to dip back into the present and past and become effective. It does so through the devoted commitment of those future citizens of the kingdom of God who out of love seek to realize that future in the present. What we value, the priorities we set, and the way we orient our lives is determined by our picture of God's eschatological rule. The vision of God's will finally brought to fulfillment in society and nature inspires us to incarnate it in every dimension of our present existence.

When we look ahead toward God's final future in which there will be no more war, it will make us ask seriously why we have to have war now. If it is in God's ultimate plan that swords are replaced by plowshares and pruning hooks, then it will bother us to have the taxes we pay used to send bullets and bombs all over the globe to people who really need wheat and rice. And we will work to change this pattern.

To look forward to a time when there will be no more mourning or crying will inspire us to root out the causes of pain and suffering in the present. If it is in God's ultimate plan that all humanity be united by a single bond of brotherhood, then we will have no truck with the vicious prejudices and selfish apathies of the affluent, who by simply ignoring the whines of the poor and hungry consign them to a miserable fate.

Looking forward to our own Easter inspires us to live as resurrected people now. This means that we incarnate in ourselves the selfless love and concern that will pervade God's rule when it becomes absolute. The absolute power of God is the power of absolute self-giving. It was proleptically embodied in the life and death of Jesus. Therefore, what we know about Jesus Christ becomes the hermeneutic vantage point from which we can understand the challenge the future of God addresses to our lives in the present. To understand what it means to live a resurrected life requires that we look to the life lived by Jesus, a life confirmed by God when he raised Jesus from the dead. Jesus is our model and inspiration.

Keeping in mind the apocalyptic vision of God's future as both altered and confirmed by the destiny of Jesus, perhaps we now have a vantage point from which we may interpret the deeper dimensions of the contemporary consciousness of the future. To that task we now turn.

4
HOPE IN THE FUTURE

"We shall overcome" sang the Atlanta congregation again and again on July 10, 1974. It was a funeral. A blast of bullets had been aimed at the Reverend Martin Luther King, Sr. during Sunday morning worship, but instead they brought bloody death to Mrs. King and a deacon. Seven years earlier the Kings' son had been murdered in a similar assassination, at the climax of more than a decade of striving for civil rights. The words, "we shall overcome someday," persistently echo a dimension of future consciousness, a dimension rooted in dissatisfaction with the present state of affairs. The present stands under judgment; it should die in favor of a resurrected future.

Future consciousness depends upon an awareness of the possibility that the future can be different from the present and past. Dissatisfaction with the present state of affairs may accentuate the distinction between present and future, especially if it is believed that the future can be better.

Desire for the new is the flip side of dissatisfaction with the present. Our Western culture, especially America, is characterized by a near-insatiable appetite for novelty. The new is identified with the good so that the passage of time is thought of in terms of progress; things are getting better and better. This desire for the new, because it is believed that the new is good, we can call "hope."

It must be added, however, that the concept of hope involves more than merely the desire for the new. To want more and better cars, houses, and gadgets could be a sign of simple consumptive lust. The accent in hope is to trust in the new rather than the old; it is not simply another form of "gimmie-gimmie." We may put the "gimmie-gimmie" obsession and hope on each end of a continuum labeled "desire for the new." As we move from one end toward the other, consumptive lust gives way to desire for a higher standard of material living, which in turn leads to a desire to satisfy material needs in order to be free to concentrate on the more interpersonal and human dimensions of life; this leads finally to a visionary hope for the consummate fulfillment of our human destiny. Thus, as we progress from the brute desire for new things to genuine hope, we also move from consumptive lust to the desire for human fulfillment, to the desire for a new level of humanity. Psychologist Erich Fromm calls it (in *The Revolution of Hope*) the desire for "greater aliveness". In theology it is known as the reign of God. Contemporary future consciousness includes the desire for the new in both of these forms: consumptive lust and hope for a new humanity.

But strictly secular or humanistic future consciousness has a built-in incoherency. I call it the *eschatological problem*. Basically, the problem is this: if we are dissatisfied with the present state of humanity and desire a new one, how can this be achieved by the human race alone? If we can blame humanity for putting us in the present mess, can we assume that the same humanity will have what it takes to get us out of the mess? If people are the problem, how can they also be the solution?

Very much in tune with secular future consciousness in general, distinctively Christian future consciousness is also dissatisfied with the present and hopeful for the new. But the eschatological problem is resolved by placing that hope in the power of God. What people are unable or unwilling to do on their own, God has promised to accomplish by *his* power. When confronted with the model of a new humanity in the person of Jesus, our ancestors chose to put him to a cruel and unjust death. That same cruelty and injustice persist today, and they will continue to persist tomorrow if we are left to determine the future solely by ourselves. The message of Easter is that cruelty and injustice and even death are not eternal. On Easter God raised the dead Jesus to victory by divine power. So also does he promise to raise humanity to a new level of being by that same divine power. To place our hope in humanity alone is to build a house on sinking sand. However, there is some solid ground upon which Christian faith can place its hope, namely, the power of God. *Futurum* is human, *adventus* divine.

DISSATISFACTION WITH THE PRESENT

The reason Charles Reich, in *The Greening of America,* looked forward to the victorious takeover of Consciousness III was that Consciousness I and II made such a mess of things. The concerns of the counterculture of the late 1960s have become the concerns of the larger society in the mid-1970s. Many are dissatisfied with present America because it is fraught with disorder, corruption, hypocrisy, and a war mentality. Not only are there race riots and muggings, but a kind of lawlessness pervades our great institutions, the government, and our large corporations. In the midst of great affluence, America has millions of people caught in a cycle of poverty, oppressed by laws and a tax structure that aids only a few wealthy people.

Uncontrolled technology has gone wild. Like a mindless bull-dozer it has swept across our land pulverizing and destroying the landscape, our natural environment, our rich traditions, and the beauty of private life. The managerial hierarchy that runs our government has stripped average people of any power to guide their own destinies. Daily work—for those who are not standing in unemployment lines—has become pointless and mindless, offering no fulfillment to the worker, so that "true living" must be sought during time off. Worst of all, America is characterized by a great loss of self. The individual is stripped of imagination, creativity, and personal uniqueness. All this is done in order to mold or style the individual into a producing unit for mass technological society.

It is this diagnosis and negative judgment upon our present state of affairs that impelled the counterculture to look forward to a revolutionary transformation that would make the future different. The revolution Charles Reich predicted would be the advent of a new way of life sweeping over humanity. He labeled it Consciousness III, and in it we would find:

Respect for each individual, for his uniqueness, and for
his privacy. Abstention from coercion or violence
against any individual, abstention from killing or war.
Respect for the natural environment. Respect for beauty
in all its forms. Honesty in all personal relations. Equality
of status between all individuals, so that no one is "superior" or "inferior." Genuine democracy in the making
of decisions, freedom of expression, and conscience.[1]

Reich's dissatisfaction with the present led him to project a kind of
utopian heaven for the future.

Without quite the pomp and flair of Charles Reich, the future
prognosticator Robert Heilbroner makes a similar analysis of what
he calls our "current anxiety" and the need for a revolutionary
change in human consciousness. But he is not nearly so optimistic
regarding the prospects of our achieving those changes. Heilbroner
describes the American mood as anxious on three counts. First of
all, a barrage of confidence-shaking events has filled us with a sense
of uneasiness and foreboding. The Vietnam War has undermined
every aspect of American life—our belief in our invincible power,
our trust in our government, our estimate of our private level of
morality. Accompanying the war abroad has been an explosion at
home of street crime, race riots, bombings, bizarre airplane hijack-
ings, kidnappings, and shocking assassinations. The television image
of middle-class American gentility has been unmasked; and we are
now forced to admit the barbarism previously hidden behind the
superficial amenities of life.[2]

The second characteristic of our current anxiety, according to
Heilbroner, involves attitudinal changes that are the result of the
events listed above—changes that are part of our unarticulated
consciousness. One such change is the loss of assurance about the
course of social events. In the last century and a half Western
culture has placed great confidence in two doctrines: social progress and human rationality. The idea of progress meant that as time
passed things would become increasingly better, thus providing a
basis for confidence in the future. But World War I and the Great
Depression battered the notion of progress for Europeans; and the
Vietnam debacle, the nationwide deterioration of the school sys-

tem, along with skyrocketing inflation are destroying it for Americans. Things are worse now than they were before, and the basis for confidence in progress is evaporating.

Tied to the doctrine of progress is the belief in human rationality. Things are supposedly progressing because our innately rational nature is enabling us to gain more and more control over ourselves and our world. Once humanity's ability to reason developed to its fullest potential, argued the nineteenth-century optimists, there would be virtually no unsolvable problems. But in recent decades we have become aware of the limits of rationality with regard to social engineering. Inflation, at least in capitalist economies, seems to be unstoppable no matter how many Ph.D. economists put their heads together. No amount of reasoning seems to be able to ameliorate the ethnic hatred between the Hindus and Moslems in India, the Jews and Arabs in the Middle East, or the blacks and whites in North America. And no matter how intelligently we engineer a system for delivering massive resources to poor people, poverty continues to persist. Explosive social problems seem to be beyond any human control; nobody is in charge. The sense of assurance and confidence in our rational ability to control ourselves is vanishing rapidly.

In addition, our ability to control the external world is in doubt; there is an increasing awareness that the quality of our surroundings and thereby the quality of our life is deteriorating. The advent of the energy crisis alerts us to the prospect of a ceiling for industrial production and an end to economic growth. Not only are we exhausting the earth's resources for sustaining life, but we are also polluting the environment, thereby making it less inhabitable.

All this leads to a third element in our current anxiety, which Heilbroner calls a "civilizational malaise." The civilizational malaise, in a word, reflects the inability of our civilization, directed as it is only towards material progress—higher incomes, better diets, miracles of medicine, triumphs of applied physics and chemistry—to satisfy the human spirit. The warnings of the ancient philosophers as to the ultimate inadequacy of material possessions have now been tested in reality and, after an initial period of euphoria, discovered to be true. People are not genuinely happy; they live day to day without fulfillment in the deeper dimensions of their lives.

Heilbroner's dissatisfaction with the present trend makes him look toward the future not with idealistic hope for a utopia but rather with despair. If population continues to grow while correspondingly the environment becomes less able to support it, an eco-catastrophe will be avoided only by the rise of totalitarian governments who would be able to exercise population control arbitrarily without being inhibited by democracy and reverence for individual rights or feelings. In any case, the future will be worse than the present unless something like Reich's Consciousness III miraculously transforms our present state of mind. Certainly Heilbroner would applaud such a revolution in consciousness, but he sees no empirical evidence to support such optimism.

Over a century ago this dissatisfaction with the present state of affairs was described by the mastermind of communism, Karl Marx, as *alienation*. As the young Marx examined modern society, he was struck by the fact that people are oppressed, enslaved, victims of poverty, war, and economic exploitation, in spite of their technological ability to put an end to these evils. He concluded that humanity must be in a state of estrangement from itself, that we are alienated from our true being. Unlike the immobilizing hopelessness of Heilbroner, Marx's dissatisfaction led him to look forward to a future in which this alienation would be overcome.

It is the private ownership of the means of production in capitalist society, separating workers from the results of their labor, that Marx believed to be the core of alienation. The work of a human is distinguished from that of other creatures—ants or termites, for example—because humans first project an image of what it is they desire to make and then proceed toward achieving the end they have creatively set for themselves. People who discover that their feet need protection project designs for pairs of shoes and then proceed to make them, then wear them. This work is truly human because it holds together in a unity the initial project, the means for accomplishing it, and the final result.

But in modern capitalist economies the division of labor fractures this unity. In mass production workers simply make things—objects—the final utility and value of which they will not share. This split is heightened when the manufacturing plant in which a person works is privately owned. This produces what the contemporary French Marxist Roger Garaudy calls the triple alienations of dispossession, depersonalization, and dehumanization. The worker is dispossessed when the plant owner is motivated to make a profit, because maximum effort by the workers yields them only minimum earnings, resulting in the growing disparity between the wealth produced by the workers and their share in it. They are depersonalized and dehumanized because in producing a commodity, they become merely a commodity themselves. On the assembly line in a mass society workers do not know for whom they are working, and in some cases may not even know the product they are producing. Ask workers today what they are making and they are likely to tell you $4.00 an hour; the concept of throwing yourself into your job is lost and people no longer find fulfillment through employment. The workers' movements and speed are dictated by the capitalistic system—not from within themselves—so that each worker becomes, in Marx's words, "a flesh and blood appendage in a machine of steel." This kind of alienation permeates the capitalist system; it will disappear only when the system disappears.[3]

Dissatisfaction with the alienation inherent in the capitalist system provoked the Marxists to project a future that would be different. In the future, the factories will be communal instead of private. Communism could be defined as the union of free people, working together toward a common goal while sharing among themselves the means of production. This would undercut the source of alienation. Roger Garaudy writes, "with communism, not only the alienations of labor, but every other form of alienation will come to an end."[4] This dissatisfaction with the present combined with the desire for the envisioned future society spawns the zeal to transform the capitalistic system. This is the task of revolution. The Marxist revolution is thought of in terms of a class struggle. The transformation is a turning upside down; the class on top is pushed down, and the class underneath is elevated, resulting in a workers' paradise. Through revolution humanity itself will usher in the age of communism and free itself from alienation.

But, we might ask, how does alienated humanity have the capacity to produce a de-alienated society? I raise this question and have called it the *eschatological problem*. Referring to Marxism (but it applies to Charles Reich as well) Wolfhart Pannenberg contends that "the peculiar difficulty of this secular eschatology is, however, the expectation that man—who, it is recognized, is alienated from his true nature—will at the same time be able to overcome his alienation by himself. Is he really able to achieve true humanity when starting with his alienated personality?"[5]

Marxism is secular and atheist, believing that this utopian future is something people can and will produce on their own. However, only the power of a transcendent God can free us from our alienation and reconcile us to ourselves. And this is promsied in the future kingdom of God. Nevertheless, with or without God, consciousness of the possibility of a new future is prompted to a large extent by dissatisfaction with the present.

PROGRESS AND THE NEW HUMANITY

Our general appetite for the new is most vividly portrayed in our habits of consumption since World War II. The great American industrial machine which tooled up to repel the aggression of Japan and Germany had a tremendous capacity for production. With the signing of the peace treaties, however, this enormous potential for mass production could no longer generate only war machinery, so it had to face the possibility that it would no longer be needed. Where could all of its produce go? The answer was found through Madison Avenue advertising. The American consumers would buy it whether they needed it or not. It became the job of the advertising industry to convince the purchasing public that it should buy everything our factories could produce. If, however, the average consumers already had the basic things they needed, i. e., food and shelter, and if they were still of the Depression and hard-work mentality which had serious reservations about living in luxury, then the question became, "on what basis can they be motivated to buy something they do not actually need?" The answer was, "because it is new!"

Whatever is new has become subtly identified with the good. Even though many families who needed a car for daily transportation already had one, and even if it was running satisfactorily, they were told it was desirable to buy another car simply because it would be a new one. In turn, the American auto manufacturers during this period modified their products each year, with full body changes every two to four years, so that they could always offer something new to their customers.

Such an advertising technique could be successful only because it strikes a vital nerve in our psychic makeup: we Westerners want the new. In his book *The Image* Daniel J. Boorstin criticizes our desire for novelty, saying that Americans suffer from "extravagant expectations." Our expectations are extravagant because we expect more novelty than the flow of world events can give us. When the real world fails to yield all the novelty we expect, we then construct illusions of the new which Boorstin calls "pseudo-events." The news media especially have been presed to meet our insatiable appetite. "The simplest of our extravagant expectations concerns the amount of novelty in the world. There was a time when the reader of an unexciting newspaper would remark, 'How dull is the world today!' Nowadays he says, 'What a dull newspaper!' "[6] The expectation on the part of the reader for constant excitement through novelty caused the news media to respond by creating news when there otherwise was none. Thus, the invention of pseudo-events.

Our desire for the new also has the power to cut our emotional and cultural ties with the old. In 1959, Mattel Incorporated introduced the Barbie Doll to the little girls of America. Since then it has sold 98,000,000 dolls. That is the equivalent of nearly half the population of the United States. Later, Mattel announced they were coming out with a new model. The new improved Barbie Doll would have a slimmer figure, real eyelashes and a twist-turn waist, which would make her appear more human than the first model. In addition, the old model Barbie Doll could be used as a trade-in on the new one. This reflects a new attitude towards things, comments Alvin Toffler: "Nothing could be more dramatic than the difference between the new breed of little girls who cheerfully turn in their Barbies for the new improved model and those who, like their mothers and grandmothers before them, clutch lingeringly and lovingly to the same doll until it disintegrates from sheer age."[7] Thus we see that the desire for the new which we are presently experiencing is sometimes stronger than past emotional affections. Prospects for the new in the future cut us loose from our attachments to the present and the past.

The ability to cut ourselves off from the past and to trust in the newness which the future is expected to bring presupposes an implicit faith in the passage of time. This faith that the passage of time will automatically bring better things than we now have is called the doctrine of progress.

"Progress is our most important product," is the claim of the General Electric Company. Our faith in progress has been so pervasive that it is almost invisible, like the water in which the fish swims. The doctrine of progress assumes that we can fulfill our destiny through technical, intellectual, and cultural development, that is, through conquering nature. And there is evidence that technical progress—even in its narrowest and most material sense—helps people to realize their goals. It has allowed us to lighten the worker's load, to broaden human relationships, and to strengthen our dominion over the natural creation.

Future consciousness for the most part expects this progress to continue, and some utopian and scientific futurists expect it to continue until the human desire for material things is satiated. Industrial production and technological advance are expected to eliminate the scarcity of goods, and this will automatically abolish all competitiveness and strife between people. R. Buckminster Fuller contends that "wars have always occurred because of the underlying inadequacy of vital supplies. We will always have war until there is enough to support all humanity."[8] This belief implies that once we are freed from dependence on material things, the situation will be ripe for a more humane rather than cutthroat form of society. However, it seems a bit naive to believe that once some of the people have sufficient material wealth to satisfy their basic needs they will be ready and willing to share their superfluities with those less fortunate. The term "affluent society" was invented to describe people who had met all their basic needs but then went on to demand more and more. The desire for the new builds obsolescence right into the marketplace so that there is no end to the demand.

As long as we have the desire for the new we will never be satisfied; consumptive lust will not allow us to be spiritually free from material things.

Karl Marx did not speculate a great deal on what his future communist society would be like, yet it is clear from every aspect of his work that one of the necessary conditions for socialism, for genuine human equality, was economic abundance.

> . . . after the productive forces have also increased with the all-around development of the individual, and all the springs of co-operative wealth flow more abundantly— only then can the narrow horizon of bourgeois right be crossed in its entirety and society inscribe on its banners: From each according to his ability, to each according to his needs.[9]

Marx assumes that material abundance satisfies basic needs and can —if private property is abolished—free us for a truly humane treatment of one another. This is a common assumption found among future prognosticators.

The great twentieth-century economist John Maynard Keynes asked back in 1930 during the worldwide Depression, "what can we reasonably expect the level of our economic life to be a hundred years hence?" The Depression, he was convinced, was a temporary side trip from the central path of progress which was really being guided by technological productivity and the sustained means for the accumulation of capital. The "magic" of compound interest had been discovered; growth could build on growth. He remarked that if capital were to increase at two percent per annum, then the capital equipment of the world will have increased by half in twenty years, and seven and a half times in a century. To Keynes this meant

> . . . in the long run *that mankind is solving its economic problem.* I would predict that the standard of life in progressive countries one hundred years hence will be between four and eight times as high as it is today. There would be nothing surprising in this even in the light of our present knowledge. It would not be foolish to contemplate far greater progress still.[10]

There are reasons why we may now "contemplate far greater progress still." During the 1960s most of the industrialized countries were growing not at two percent per annum but at three percent or more; West Germany and Italy were growing at four percent and Japan at seven percent a year. With these rates of growth accompanied by other factors, the Harvard sociologist Daniel Bell has begun describing our future in terms of a *post-industrial society.* This is to be contrasted first with a *pre-industrial society,* i. e., one still occupied with its battle to extract sustenance and wealth from nature through agriculture, fishing, and mining, and which is low in productivity; and to be contrasted second with *industrial society,* i. e., one centered on human-machine relationships, using natural sources of energy and material to manufacture goods. Post-industrial society is the next phase, and it centers on relationships between persons: information processing, intellectual advance, and service-oriented professions. It will be the age of full technology. The battle against nature will be behind us, and for those who treasure the "higher things" in life it should provide a real opportunity to foster more genuine and intense interhuman relationships. Bell describes Asia, Africa, and Latin America as pre-industrial; Western Europe, the Soviet Union, and Japan as industrial; and the United States as emerging post-industrial.[11]

With this in mind, Herman Kahn and his associates at the Hudson Institute made projections of the world's economies to the year 2000. Until the last two or three centuries no large human society has ever produced more than the equivalent of $200 per capita annually, but by the year 2000 more than five-sixths of the world will have broken out of this range. At that time, Kahn estimates, there will be twelve countries that will be visibly post-industrial and nine countries in the early post-industrial stage. Income in the United States will triple to more than $10,000 per person (in 1965 dollars) as against the $3,550 per person in 1965. Leisure will increase as required working time drops to four days per week with a 13-week per year vacation. Life will be good and getting better. Kahn looks forward to America's quadricentennial in 2176 as a time of great abundance, with a Gross World Product of $300 trillion, reduced competition, greater travel and contact, diminished antagonism between peoples, and a relative lack of violence and war. The abundant life of the post-industrials will be marred only by the knowledge on the part of the morally sensitive that it will not be shared with everyone; the absolute gap between the rich and the poor will widen so that we will find "a rather large island of wealth surrounded by 'misery.'"[12]

The implicit belief seems to be that with increased affluence people will become freed from their preoccupations with satisfying their own material wants. This new freedom is supposed to lead us toward concern for matters of the spirit, the human needs for affection and purpose in life. By satisfying the material wants of the self, selfishness itself is somehow supposed to be transcended.

This implicit optimism toward human nature becomes explicit in some futurists. The University of Michigan biophysicist John R. Platt foresees the continuing progress of technology leading us toward a higher plateau of evolution, where the dangerous competition between individuals will give way to a unity of all people. He calls it the "step to man." Because of technology, Platt says, we now realize we are not running out of energy as we had thought, but have fission and fusion power enough for millions of years. The earth is ours, we have reached its ends; and our satellites have begun to range the solar system and take people to the moon. We have begun to acquire the biological keys to life and death with the increasing elimination of disease and the potential control of our own population and with the beginnings of the chemical manipulation of heredity. "And all over the globe," he writes, "we have suddenly discovered we are one society, indivisible, for life or death."[13]

Humanity is in the process of growing up, of attaining a desirably new level of maturity. The key to this maturing process Platt believes is education. In the last century or two, since Rousseau and Pestalozzi and Montessori, leaders have begun to think seriously about how they could change society systematically by changing the education of the children. Platt is intrigued by the discoveries of behavioristic psychology with regard to learning. He refers to the experiments of B. F. Skinner at Harvard who, by using the method of "rapid-reinforcement" without any punishment, trained dogs and pigeons to do tricks that dogs and pigeons allegedly never did in the history of the world before. Now human beings, with these rapid teaching methods and with "programmed teaching" based upon them, can likewise learn many things faster and easier than has been possible with older methods. This power to determine a child's behavior through "good teaching," of course, could be directed toward either good or evil purposes. Those purposes we will have to choose, but the power to achieve them is rapidly becoming available. "There have been many revolutions in our time," writes Platt, "but I think that in the long run this psychological revolution that we see beginning here in the theory and practice of shaping behavior of the young will be the most important revolution of all for the success and happiness of man on this planet."[14]

Human nature is not constant but rather is in a process of continual change, argues Platt, so that education even has the capacity to cleanse people of their evil ways and help us achieve world harmony. To some extent it has already done so. People are more humane today than yesterday. He points out that we moderns can be contrasted with our medieval ancestors for whom the torture of humans and animals was a daily feature of life. Trial by combat and dueling as methods of deciding the rights and wrongs of a civil dispute are no longer accepted. After alluding to the death camps of Germany a few decades ago, he says, "the mass of mankind repudiates them today."[15] Platt believes humanity is showing a new level of purpose and design, a new feeling that we are morally responsible for ourselves. This in conjunction with the discovery that it is culture that shapes our minds and actions—that better education leads to better actions—enables us to make a new world. There is an incredible amount of social engineering yet to be done, to make social structures that will give us freedom and yet keep us from killing each other, but it is now clear that it can be done.

Platt compares the present crucial "hinge of history" in the evolution toward maturity among the human race with riding a bicycle. The first time the child straddles a two-wheeler it seems terribly scary, and perhaps there is a fall accompanied by a skinned knee or elbow. But the child gets up again, the parent holds the handlebars, running along beside; and suddenly the child is riding alone. At one instant the child is incompetent, falling to one side or the other and steering wrong. The next instant it comes right and the driver is in control, safe and balanced. Wobbling and weaving eventually give way to a path that is straight and true. In like manner, Platt believes that by the year 2000 the human race may emerge from its time of wobbling conflict and uncertainty over falling, and it will suddenly be riding in its own chosen direction, free, as only a coordinated and confident organism can be.[16]

> I believe it quite likely that we may evolve from one kind
> of future to another over the centuries, once we learn
> the basic social rules that will keep us from collective
> self-destruction. . . . Human nature is growing up. As we
> put behind us the accidents and tears of childhood
> squabbles and the wooden swords and shields, and
> begin to try on our new space-pilot's uniform, so to
> speak, we begin to see what we can teach ourselves
> and what we can really become with new self-control
> over our new adult powers.[17]

Platt is saying that *futurum* alone is going to cure our selfishness and that evolutionary progress will eventually transform humanity from sinner into saint. The precedents and powers necessary to bring about the new we desire are fully extant in present trends, and their future realization is *almost* automatic.

Victor Ferkiss also looks forward to the coming of a new stage in human development; he calls it "technological man."[18] He agrees with Daniel Bell that the context will be a post-industrial and more purely technological era; he agrees with John Platt that human nature can change and that we are presently at the hinge of history where humanity is about to take control of its own evolution through technology. However, Ferkiss does not think that this next step in human evolution will be automatic. There is no guarantee that it will take place at all. This is due to the very nature of the step: if the direction of evolutionary progress comes under the control of a human race that possesses free will, then humanity is free to either shoulder the responsibility or not.

We are moving beyond industrial into a post-industrial situation, but Ferkiss fears that the values and norms that directed human behavior during the liberal industrial period will be inappropriately carried on over into the new era. Daniel Bell optimistically characterizes the post-industrial society as one that will be dominated by a small highly trained technical elite who will be motivated and directed by the high-minded ideals of science; the university will be the institution at the center of the society of the future.[19] Would that it were so, pines Ferkiss, but the evidence is not yet conclusive in Bell's favor. At present, our well-paid technical experts do play important roles, but their standards do not predominate. Their economic position, and hence their contribution to society as a whole, is controlled by the continuing dominance of the corporate head whose mores and laws are holdovers from the industrial-bourgeois era. The evidence is not in favor of the thesis that the university is moving toward the center of society: enrollments are falling, staff salaries are losing pace with the economy, bankruptcy is staring many institutions in the face, and there is a creeping general disillusionment over the contribution of higher learning to the average citizen's welfare.

The values concomitant with liberal industrial society included the attitude that work was the proper end of each individual (the so-called Protestant Ethic), that we were meant to exploit nature and compete with others for our own purposes, that invention and progress are good. But all of these converge on the basic motivation, namely, the selfish drive for power and wealth. The basic law of economics was either to dominate or be dominated, whether the competitive struggle was a struggle against nature or against other people. But as we move toward the post-industrial era, we find that our technological power makes us capable of genetically altering the whole human race or even eliminating it entirely through biological or nuclear warfare. We are rapidly becoming a single planetary society where we can no longer afford competition either between ourselves and nature or between ourselves and others. With this newly attained power, the industrial and bourgeois value of gaining power over one's competitor portends destruction.

> The central danger facing humankind in the latter part of the twentieth century lies not in the autonomy of technology or in the triumph of technological values but in the subordination of technology to the values of earlier historical eras and its exploitation by those who

do not understand its implications and consequences but
seek only their own selfish personal or group purposes.
The new man with his vast powers is coming into existence as the servant of neoprimitive man.[20]

Ferkiss desires a new kind of person at a higher stage of human
evolution—a stage we are all looking for—when technology will
serve human purposes, when abundance, peace, and cooperation
will be shared by the whole human race. But Ferkiss is clear that this
is a "hope and not a promise." ("Technological man" is not the
inhuman robot that some superficial readers of Ferkiss interpret;
Ferkiss has admitted, however, that the title of his first book, *Technological Man,* may have been misleading in this regard.)

Now let us see where we have been. We have begun with basic
consumptive lust as it implicitly identifies the new with the good. But
this is part of a wider and deeper belief in the doctrine of progress,
that as time passes the future will bring better things than the past.
And as the doctrine of progress begins to move beyond basic
material concerns toward the higher values appropriate to the
human condition—cooperation, not competition; unity, not division;
peace, not conflict; humanity over the machine—our bald trust in
progress begins to waver. We want to believe that a renewed
humanity is just the next stage in evolutionary progress, but we are
not sure that that stage will come automatically. That stage, unfortu-
nately, is contingent upon what we decide to do. Our desire for a
new humanity becomes a "hope," not a "promise."

HOPE FOR THE FUTURE

"Hope is as necessary for human life as oxygen," writes the
Lutheran theologian Hans Schwarz.[21] It is part of the dynamic of a
person's nature to hope. Erich Fromm, the psychoanalyst, says that
"hope is an intrinsic element of the structure of life, of the dynamic
of man's spirit."[22]

Without hope directed toward a positive future the present
becomes unlivable. The emotional state of a prisoner, for example,
is dependent upon what that prisoner expects will happen in the
future. Psychological studies have shown that prisoners are far more
likely to suffer from depression if there is uncertainty about their

projected time of parole or release or if there is no hope of making a break. These are far more potent factors determining their state of mind than are the day-to-day factors such as satisfaction with prison jobs.[23] If the future is not meaningful, James Cone submits, "all is despair."[24]

For each of us, to live without hope is to be imprisoned in the present. To be deprived of hope is to lose the freedom to go beyond the present. It is hope in the face of an open future that makes freedom possible. Without it we would find ourselves in bondage to past traditions and present predicaments.

This implies at least two things. First, what is sought from the future is something qualitatively new. Hope sees the future as holding possibilities that are not merely extensions of past trends or a continuation of the present state of affairs. If that were the case, then belief in progress would suffice without hope. But hope incorporates doubt within it. Maybe it will not come to pass! To "hope against hope" is to recognize that the new which I desire is not merely the expected outcome of present trends. In fact, the direction things are presently taking might even be contrary to the object of our hope. Hope's vision of the future is implicity *adventus*.

Thus, when John Platt and Victor Ferkiss—it is much more clear in Ferkiss—speak of the "step to man" or "technological man," they are hoping. The advance to the new humanity is desired, to be sure, but it cannot be expected to come automatically. The new humanity is *new* for just this reason: it is different from the humanity we presently know. The precedents are meager. To simply expect that the step to the new humanity will be taken automatically would be naive, though Platt sometimes borders on this naiveté. Consequently, Ferkiss calls it a "hope" for something very new rather than a "promise" based upon present realities.

This leads to the second implication, namely, that the present is judged to be evil. It is not necessarily totally depraved, but it is certainly less good than that for which we hope. Without the negative interpretation of the present situation hope would be meaningless. Hope lives in the tension between the negative elements of the present and the positive expectations of the future.

Here is the eschatological problem once again: how do we get there from here? Platt's "step to man" and Ferkiss's "technological man," just like Reich's Consciousness III and Marx's eschatological communism, project a new humanity which we cannot expect to appear on the basis of humanity's present record. It is just because we now have liberal industrial society—replete with selfish competition, a rapacious appetite for devouring nature, and set policies which are hurling us toward self-destruction—that Ferkiss hopes for the advent of "technological man" to save us from ourselves. "Technological man" will stand in sharp contrast with the present; it will not come as the automatic product of evolutionary development. Then by what power will it come? By what means will present humanity be transformed into the new humanity? To hope that people can do it alone is really to hope against hope. It is certainly no more absurd to hope that a divine force in the future will fulfill a promise to redeem us than it is to hope that, unredeemed, we will do it alone. Is there not built right into the structure of hope itself that which Christian theology has referred to as our desire for salvation?

It is interesting to note that a prominent contemporary Marxist contends that hope is implicitly a religious phenomenon. Ernst Bloch says, "Where there is hope, there is religion."[25] Following Bloch, Carl Braaten writes, "Where there is life, there is hope, and where there is hope, there is religion."[26] Insofar as hope is an expectation that includes the element of doubt, insofar as it includes the recognition that the future for which we are hoping lies beyond our own powers to attain, then it takes on a religious character. It begins to place faith in an ultimate power greater than ourselves. Hope, then, is finally a question to which grace is the answer. By "grace," theology refers to the inclination of the divine power to give us what we ourselves are unable or unwilling to achieve on our own, especially the forgiveness of sins and eternal life. Thus Karl Rahner writes, "in the case of non-Christians the ultimate motive force behind their acts and decisions as a part of human history is still, even in their case, precisely *grace,* even though they do not recognize it."[27] Hope for a new humanity is implicitly a request for divine grace, and grace is received through faith.

Hence, hope is closely allied to faith. Erich Fromm agrees that hope and faith are closely allied, and he designates faith as that which supplies the *knowledge* needed for hope. Hope is not simply a flying leap into the utter openness of the future, rather it is based upon faith's knowledge of real possibilities. Fromm says that "Faith like hope, is not prediction of the *future,* it is the vision of the *present* in a state of pregnancy."[28] In a sense, then, the future for faith is *futurum.*

Let me define faith as trust in the future, or more precisely, trust in the God of the future. Faith is not blind trust. It is trust in something in particular, and it knows about that in which it places its trust. Faith depends upon a past revelation of that extra-human power in order to specify its hope for the future. There must be a precedent in the past upon which we can base our hope. Of course, our past is loaded with precedents for many things, i. e., there are many influential trends that lead future forecasters to project alternative futures. It is of little relevance whether the precedent that gives rise to our hope is a dominant or obscure trend, but it must be there already before it can support a faith in the future. At least in this sense, hope and faith must see "the present in a state of pregnancy."

What precedent is there presently available for us, then, that can support a faith and a hope for a new humanity? Answer: the knowledge of what the God of the future has done already in Jesus Christ. Jesus Christ differs from ordinary humanity in that he is the eschatological new humanity made actual in his own person and career. He is the precedent and the promise of what is to come for us in the future.

Faith and hope are anchored in their witness to the third item in Paul's famous trilogy, love. The zenith of love for God and for human beings has been concretely manifested in the teachings and devoted career of Jesus. In Jesus we see some of the characteristics of the new humanity we desire: concern, not competition; healing, not hating; donating, not dominating; loving, not lusting; self-giving and forgiving, not giving to self. Jesus attains the new humanity because he shares essential unity with the God of the future, the extra-human power without whom the new humanity can never become a concrete reality.

5
TIME AND HISTORY

Future consciousness depends upon a particular kind of time consciousness. This understanding of time is what we call linear or historical time, that is, time that moves in a one-directional line from a beginning toward an end. This notion of time is characterized by the one-after-the-otherness of events. Each event is understood as being unique and happening once and for all. No event can ever be repeated in exactly the same way that it first occurred. This means then that the future is open for new events which have no complete precedents in the past. Because the future is open to new and more or less unique events with their own integrity, no one can know precisely what will occur in the future. We can only face the future with hope or fear.

Linear time is embedded deep in our modern consciousness. It is common to say we are "behind the times" or "it is later than you think." We have proverbs such as "life can be understood only backward, but it must be lived forward." Second only to love, time is the most prevalent theme in the great literature and poetry of the West. The often sung hymn by Isaac Watts based on Psalm 90, "O God, Our Help in Ages Past," includes the following stanzas:

Time, like an ever-rolling stream,
Bears all its sons away;
They fly forgotten as a dream
Dies at the opening day.

O God, our Help in ages past,
Our Hope for years to come,

Be Thou our Guard while life shall last,
And our eternal Home.

The natural sciences assume time is linear, moving from past to future. Geology traces the development of the earth through successive stages over a span of millions of years. Biology traces the evolution of various species of life, presenting the human race we know today as a not-yet-final product of a long line of development from earlier living organisms.

And even more obviously than the natural sciences, the study of human history pictures and locates what happens along a one-directional time scale. We have a dating measure which orients all events to a single temporal continuum. Alexander the Great died in the year 323 B.C., and this occurred before the Battle of Hastings (A.D. 1066), which in turn was followed by the signing of the American Declaration of Independence in A.D. 1776. And the present stands between what has happened and what is to come.

Everyone is traveling into the future at the steady speed of twenty-four hours every day. But each day brings changes with it. Because we understand the future to be a further extension of a line stretching from the past into the present, we can forecast changes for tomorrow. We cannot stop along this line, so to many of us today the apparent inevitability of change appears overwhelming. Time becomes terrifying.

IS TIME RUNNING OUT?

"Change, change, change, continual change. This is the watchword of modern life," writes John R. Platt.[1] Nothing stands still. Everything is transient. But even more than that, for many our destiny of change means that today the forces which govern and direct the changes we are undergoing are temporarily out of control. We are caught in a stampede of change; there is an avalanche carrying us along and we are doing nothing to determine its direction. For good or ill, the power of the future is carrying us where it wills.

Alvin Toffler takes this basic perspective. The very title of his widely read book *Future Shock* indicates that it deals with people's reactions to a future they cannot control. The introduction opens by saying, "This is a book about what happens to people when they are overwhelmed by change."[2] Note the use of the passive construction. It is not basically a book about how people make change, but rather, given change, what happens to people when they respond to it. The chapter subtitles reflect the feeling that change is our destiny and that humanity is caught in the stampede: "Response to Novelty," "The Adaptive Reaction," "Victims of Future Shock." Toffler sums up his thesis, "Future shock is the dizzying disorientation brought on by the premature arrival of the future."[3] People are presently so overstimulated by such an overwhelming bombardment of novelty that their biological and psychic systems are unable to react and adapt appropriately. Change and novelty are our destiny; if we cannot adapt, the result is future shock.

As to whether or not we can adapt, in the minds of many today there is only the slimmest possible hope. The facts diminish hope. First, the exponential growth of population projected toward a grotesque twenty billion people by the year 2050, coupled with even the most optimistic projections of increased food production through improved fertilizers, means only famine for the future. Second, the spread of nuclear potential to the developing countries may lead to policies of nuclear terrorism against the developed nations—the underdeveloped face starvation and so have nothing to lose. Third, the ecosphere is rapidly losing its ability to support human life because it is caught in a cross fire between exhaustion of natural resources on the one hand and pollution on the other.

Thus, despite the optimistic projections of the previous chapter, for many the twenty-first century looks grim. If we examine more closely the trajectory of present trends, we can see why some scientists believe that the human race is being hurled toward cataclysmic self-destruction. The rate of growth in population, accompanied by an even higher rate of growth in industrial production and its accompanying pollution, is inevitably leading to a showdown in which people will either starve due to the exhaustion of earth's resources or else be poisoned to death wallowing in their own pollution. Before reaching that point we may destroy ourselves in a war between the haves and have-nots over the few remaining unpolluted resources. We and our children seem to be caught in this irreversible eddy; and what makes it so tragic is that we know what can and must be done to halt it.

As mentioned above, population is now growing exponentially. Exponential growth refers to the doubling effect when two parents have four children, each of whom in turn produces twice as many progeny. For much of the world's history, the population grew steadily but not at this dramatic exponential rate. It took all of the world's history for the human race to grow to the population of one billion by the year 1830. But then things began to change, most probably due to advances in scientific medicine and sanitation practices. A hundred years later, in 1930, it had doubled to two billion. By 1975 or so, only 45 years later, it had doubled again to nearly four billion. The largest growth during this period is to be found in the developing nations where malaria control and other medical advances have had a great impact. And if present fertility rates hold, the people of the earth will number 7.5 billion at the turn of the century, and after that we can add about one billion people every five years.

It is important to note that this growth is not evenly distributed throughout the world. The industrialized areas such as the United States and Europe are not growing as fast as the poorer peoples of Asia and Latin America. The population growth rate of the industrial countries is about 1% per year, while it is between 2.5% and 3.5% per year for the developing countries. Over the last two centuries we have witnessed a decline in birth rates in the industrial West. It seems that parents in the affluent countries generally decide to have smaller families. When the United States was born in 1776, the average American woman gave birth to eight children. In 1900 she bore only four children, and at present she is averaging about two. In order to achieve zero population growth, each married woman would have to average 2.11 children (the extra .11 to account for single people not bearing children). Even though the birth rate has declined, the population has increased because fewer people die each year due to improved diet and health care. Because birth rates have declined in both Europe and America, we must attribute our more modest population growth to declining death rates alone.

But the story is different in the less developed countries, where most of the world's people now live and where the death rates have declined while the birth rates remained high. Prior to the present era, the traditional birth rate of Third World countries was 40 to 50 per 1000 people per year. The corresponding death rate was about 38 per 1000, which produced a continual but gradual increase. During the second quarter of the twentieth century increased public sanitation, the sudden widespread availability of modern medicine, and massive programs to stamp out malaria have resulted in substantial reductions in death rates. The death rate has dropped to 15 to 18 per 1000, but the birth rate has remained constant. When asked why they have eight or more children, Third World parents answer that even though some of the children will die along the way, they want to guarantee that some will survive to care for them in their old age. The governments of these nations spit on U. N. suggestions that they should enforce birth control, arguing that the plan is a plot by the wealthy industrial nations to prevent their becoming outnumbered by the poorer peoples. It is these circumstances that have produced the explosion in the world's population.

The burgeoning population of the world would cause no alarm if there were some guarantee that the earth's resources could produce enough food to eat and that the processing of these resources would not pollute us to death. But there are no such guarantees. Dr. Norman E. Borlaug, winner of the Nobel Prize for developing the "miracle" strains of wheat and rice that produced the Green Revolution in Mexico and elsewhere, says population is growing at such a rate that even the most widespread use of higher yield fertilizer conceivable will not be able to keep pace with the hungry mouths. In addition, we can already project the exhaustion of some natural resources, and present projections regarding pollution are even more gloomy.

A group of scientists and scholars who have studied systems dynamics with Jay W. Forrester at MIT and who call themselves the Club of Rome have taken a systems-analysis approach to just these problems. In their very important book *The Limits to Growth* they attempt to project the future of the whole world by examining the interaction between the five basic factors that determine growth on

our planet—population, agricultural production, nonrenewable natural resource depletion, industrial production, and pollution.[4]

One very significant feature of the Club of Rome study is the use
of a world model.[5] The growth factors just listed are mutually
interdependent and function as a single system. Population growth
affects resource use, which in turn affects the amount of pollution,
which in turn rebounds to affect population growth. A change in the
pattern of one factor is necessarily reflected in the patterns of all
the others. By implication, the Club has accepted the fact that finally
there will be only one future for the entire world.

The Club of Rome examined present trends for each of the
factors and then fed the data into a computer a number of different
ways in order to project alternative forecasts of humanity's future.
Their first computer run showed a collapse of economic growth
within a hundred years due to the exhaustion of natural resources;
food supplies would fail because fertilizer requirements could not be
met. On the second computer run, they assumed the possibility of
discovering new natural resources, so they doubled the amount of
known resources. But in this simulation the world economy collapsed
due to excessive pollution. On the third run, where a three-quarter
reduction in the pollution rate was assumed, the simulation model
showed a continuation of economic growth for some time, but the
consequent expansion of cities and industries used up agricultural
land so that the food supply dried up. Finally, they assumed a
doubling of agricultural yields which hastened a huge industrial
expansion, but this was followed by a new collapse due to unman-
ageable pollution.

The conclusion is sobering, to say the least. Under even the most
optimistic yet reasonably realistic assumptions, our global system of
life cannot support the present exponential rates of economic and
population growth beyond the year 2100, and equally realistic but
more pessimistic assumptions forecast gigantic disasters shortly after
the year 2000. Such disasters would take the form of either mass
famine due to insufficient food production or else poisoning due to
excessive pollution.

In this regard, the model of the world system could be compared
to making wine. Winemakers are quite familiar with the exponential

growth of yeast, which grows until it meets its limit and then virtually pollutes itself to death. Along with fruit juice and water, the wine-maker places yeast and sugar into a piece of crockery; this solution is called must. In the fermentation process the yeast feeds upon the sugar which causes it to grow through cell-division, that is, each cell divides into two cells, then those two cells divide into four, and so on. This is exponential growth.

However, one of the byproducts of this process—sought after by the wine drinker—is alcohol. The more the yeast consumes the sugar and grows, the more alcohol is produced. But alcohol is deadly to yeast. The upper limit of alcohol production in any crock of must is about 12%, because when it reaches that point it kills the yeast. When the yeast is dead then alcohol is no longer produced.

If we were to liken yeast to human population, sugar to natural resources, and alcohol to pollution, the wine fermenting process provides us with a model for understanding where exponential growth is taking the world. As population grows exponentially, so does its use of natural resources and its production of pollution. If the resources do not give way first, the pollution will eventually put an end to population by poisoning it to death. In the words of Kenneth Vaux, "our world is joyously riding some uncontrolled roller coaster to impending catastrophe."[6]

With regard to those people whom the earth can feed between now and the future limit to our planet's growth, the economic problems are hastening the day of reckoning. The traditional approach to increasing food production is to expand the area of land under cultivation. But obviously this has only limited scope for the future, because eventually we will run out of land. The arable land that we do have can be farmed only if sufficient water is available for agriculture, and most of the world's rivers that lend themselves to damming and to irrigation have already been developed. In the United States over fifty million acres of cropland were idled during the 1960s because they were not needed. The food crisis of 1966–67 brought a small portion back into production. By 1974 virtually all fifty million acres were back in production and the total food reserves hit their lowest level since 1961.

With expansion of the area of land under cultivation approaching its limit, we must look to the intensification of food production on the existing cultivated area. But with the rising price of energy, the cost of fertilizer will rise commensurately. This is due in part to the fact that nitrogen fertilizer—the most widely used chemical fertilizer—is made from natural gas or petroleum, and in part because the manufacturing process consumes large amounts of energy. In addition, the price of additional increases in productivity of already high-yield land climbs sharply. For example, raising the yields of corn in the United States from ninety to one hundred bushels requires a much larger quantity of nitrogen than was needed to raise yields from fifty to sixty bushels. Both the quantity of fertilizer demanded and the price paid for it in the remaining years of this century will soar to phenomenal levels.[7]

The lack of availability of food for hungry mouths is due not only to the simple increase in the number of people as a whole, but it is complicated by the fact that the rich minority is taking an increasingly disproportionate share. The average North American consumes five times as much as the average resident of India, and that ratio is widening. You will eat nearly one ton of grain or its equivalent in meat products each year if you live in the United States, but you will eat only 400 pounds if you live in India, Nigeria, or Colombia. Meat eating is a luxury only affluent people can afford very often. Seven pounds of grain are needed to produce one pound of beef, four pounds of grain for one pound of pork, and three pounds of grain for one pound of chicken. Residents of poorer countries must either eat the more efficient forms of meat or else eat the grain directly, because grain diverted for meat production in the future competes with that needed to keep someone alive today. Harvard nutritionist Jean Mayer says that the same amount of food that is feeding 210 million Americans would feed one and a half billion Chinese on an average Chinese diet.

And the affluent appetite is increasing: the annual per capita beef consumption in the United States grew continuously from 55 pounds in 1940 to 117 pounds in 1972, where it seems to have leveled off. Citizens of the United States, Western Europe, and Australia now consume on the average between 200 and 250 pounds of meat of all kinds each year. They probably do so because they like meat's taste. It is also a status symbol of a high standard of living, even in Communist countries. When Russia suffered a crop shortfall in 1972, they did not slaughter cattle to conserve grain but rather imported 28 million tons of corn, wheat, and soybeans, in order to feed the livestock and maintain their eating habits.

Many people in the industrial West eat much more meat than is nutritionally necessary. The American Heart Association has become convinced that there is a relationship between the rise in consumption of livestock products, particularly the fattier meats, and the incidence of coronary heart disease among Americans. It is now recommended that Americans reduce per capita meat consumption by about one third strictly for health reasons.

The economist Lester Brown recommends that Western peoples alter their eating habits by becoming semi-vegetarians and eating the meats that use grain more efficiently in order to permit a more even distribution of food worldwide.[8] But this does not seem to be occurring. Whereas some of us die prematurely of coronary disease induced by overeating, others face premature death from starvation —the consequence of the disproportionate claims we make on the world's food resources.[9] In his stirring environmental scenario "Ecocatastrophe" Paul Ehrlich imagines a future meeting of the U. N. General Assembly and a speech by the ambassador from India. After pointing out that the United States, with only six percent of the world's people, consumes roughly fifty percent of its raw materials every year, he says "the birth of an American baby is a greater disaster for the world than that of twenty-five Indian babies."[10]

It is said that in a country where there are long foodlines the government will soon fall. People will not remain hungry without a fight. During the hard times of 1974, food riots became commonplace in vast sections of Bangladesh and India. The competition between rich and poor for the world's food resources could lead to a calamitous war before the earth-wide limits to growth are reached. The continuation of the present competition between rich and poor indicates a failure of vision, a failure to see that we have one world with only one future. The very failure to grasp this vision may itself be the force that breaks the dike and prematurely drowns our chances for survival.

CYCLICAL TIME VERSUS HISTORICAL TIME

The above are not *predictions* of the future; they are *forecasts.* Scientific futurists and social critics accept the fact that no one can predict in detail what will happen in the future. The future is too mysterious for that. They do, however, make forecasts. Such a forecast examines present trends and then projects possible developments based upon these trends. Of course, these future developments are contingent on a number of factors, some of which are as yet unforeseen. Thus, futurists are accustomed to forecasting alternative futures, i. e., scenarios that could go one way or another depending upon certain human choices and related developments.

These forecasts are very important in themselves. But for the moment I would like to consider them in a special way, as examples of time consciousness. Despite the gravity of the content of such projections into the future, let us pause to examine the concept of time implicit in the kind of thinking that can make such prognostications. Interestingly enough, the notion of time that is presupposed here comes into our modern consciousness from the Bible. Perhaps an examination of this concept of time will provide a link between Christian eschatology and secular futurology.

Future forecasting depends upon the concept of progressive or dynamic time. This concept of time as a linear succession of events continuing right on into a not-yet-fully-known future is so much a part or our thinking in the modern Western world that we take it for granted. However, not all peoples of all times and places have understood time in this way. In fact, primitive peoples and much of the contemporary world down to the present era have understood time as cyclical rather than linear. Furthermore, to be modern means, among other things, to accept the linear view of time and reject the cyclical.

According to the premodern view, time moves in cycles. Events can be repeated, at least in essence. What really matters is eternity, and time as we know it in human history is just a dirty mirror that occasionally reflects the eternal principles. The principles that govern the universe are fixed and final, so human time cannot expect to produce anything fully new at the ontological level, at the level of being itself.

Cyclical time is characteristic of cultures imbued with myth and ritual. Myths are narratives or stories of how some divine beings created the world at some primal time in the past, *in illo tempore,* which explains why the world is the way it is today. Because myths are genuine attempts to explain the real world as we experience it, to define myth as a story that is untrue misses the mark. In religious ritual, the worshipers dramatically repeat the events of the divine creation. But this manner of worship is not merely a way of remembering what happened in the past; it is a way of *reactualizing* the past, of making that event contemporary with the present. Through a ritual repetition of the myth, the worshipers actually participate with the gods in their creative activity. The creation of the world is not merely past, it is also present in the moment of the ritual. The ritual sharing of divine activity on the part of the worshiper serves to sanctify the present moment in time by tying it to *illud tempus,* the eternal time of the gods. The drive in myth-oriented religion is away from the future and back toward the past, because the past is the ground of being and source of meaning.

According to the mythical-cylclical view of the world, time repeats itself. The notion that present history can be abolished and that the world can be created anew follows closely the cycle of the year. The seasons of the year—spring followed relentlessly by summer, fall, and winter—are regularly repeated so that archaic societies dependent upon agriculture and hunting attune themselves to the apparent rhythms of the cosmos. Every year the cycle starts all over again. In a number of North American Indian languages one and the same term is used for our two words "cosmos" and "year." The Yokuts say "the world has passed," meaning "a year has gone by." Mircea Eliade, the great historian of religions, says that for archaic people "the cosmos is conceived as a living unity that is born, develops, and dies on the last day of the year, to be reborn on New Year's Day."[11]

Let us look briefly at an example. In the ancient Babylonian myth of creation, *Enuma Elish,* the world is created out of a battle between two gods, Marduk and Tiamat. Back in the time before there was any time, *in illo tempore,* there is just Tiamat and her husband, Apsu. All of reality is simply a chaotic mass of swirling water with

Tiamat, the she monster or dragon, representing the salt water of the ocean, and Apsu, representing the sweet water of inland fertility. The marriage of Tiamat and Apsu produces hundreds of other gods as children. The younger divinities are full of vitality and the clamoring noise of their jostling about greatly disturbs the peace of Tiamat and Apsu. The annoyed parents secretly plot to kill their progeny in order to put a halt to the hubbub. But one of them, Ea, discovers the plan and kills Apsu. Tiamat, now even more angered by the slaying of her husband, threatens war on the entire universe. Ea, trembling with fear, searches for someone to defend the gods and rescue them from the wrath of the sea monster. Marduk steps forward and volunteers his services but only at a high price: that he be king over all the gods. The agreement is made and Marduk goes to battle against Tiamat. He catches her in his net and calls upon the four winds who drive themselves into her body so that she is unable to close her lips. Marduk then thrusts his spear through the open mouth and into her heart. Following the victory, he cuts the dragon's dead body in two, lays half of it down flat, which becomes the earth, and the other half he stretches canopy-fashion over the top to become the sky. Upon the surface of the earth he creates humans, who along with the other gods are supposed to sing praises and honor to their divine king, Marduk. Dramatically told, the mythical story says that the process of creation is one of making order out of chaos.

Every spring in the land of ancient Babylonia the Tigris and Euphrates rivers overflow their banks, inundating the landscape for miles. There is destruction and chaos due to the untamed mass of swirling waters. The orderly cosmos is threatened by a return to chaos. But within the chaos is the potential for creativity; rich silt is left upon the riverbanks from which the life-giving crops will grow in the summer. A new year has begun.

The ancient Babylonians celebrated the coming of the New Year with a twelve-day festival called *akitu*.[12] During the ceremonies, groups of actors including the king would dramatically portray the story of the myth. The combat between Marduk and the sea monster Tiamat was reactualized in the drama and in this way the ritual worshipers participated with the gods themselves in the re-creation of the world for the new year. The old year was abolished in the symbolic return to chaos and the new year was brought into being. It was expected to happen again the next year. Scholars believe that what was true for the ancient Babylonians was true for archaic people in general.

This understanding of the annual renewal of the cosmos is still present with us today, even though it is scarcely recognizable. Our New Year's Eve celebrations begin with a return to chaos: symbolized by wild revelry that takes us back to human behavior prior to any moral order. At the stroke of twelve we have the feeling that we can begin things all over again, and so we announce our New Year's resolutions.

Even the shift from mythical thinking to rational thinking in ancient Greece did not advance people's apprehension of time beyond the cyclical view of myth. In his *Timaeus* (22–25), Plato saw world history as a grand cycle of rising civilizations destroyed one after the other by floods. In the *Statesman* (269–275), he says that God remains eternally the same but human history passes through repeated epochs involving "infinite cycles of years." For Plato, the human soul separated itself from the body at death in order to be born in another reincarnation, and it continued eternally on a cycle of rebirth. Humans, accordingly, had no definite aim and no real future. The classical Greek historians, Herodotus, Thucydides, and Polybius, wrote chronicles of human events, but they always sought the underlying motif of the uniform character of history due to the uniformity of human nature. For the Greeks the future could not be important because it could not bring anything essentially new. Of the ancient Greeks June Goodfield and Stephen Toulmin write, "For all the rationality of their concepts, they never put down firm intellectual roots into the temporal development of Nature, nor could they grasp the timescale of Creation with any more certainty than men had done before. . . . one may justly speak of their theories as 'rational myths.' "[13]

In myth-oriented societies time has no open future. Eventually we end up back where we started. Of archaic cultures Eliade says, "there is everywhere a conception of the end and the beginning of a temporal period, based on the observation of biocosmic rhythms."[14] If cyclical rhythm is our initial apprehension of time, then from where do modern people get the notion of linear time? The answer is the Judeo-Christian tradition.

Although it is still being debated, most scholars agree that the concept of linear time derives from the Bible.[15] The awareness of historical movement was awakened in people when they found themselves standing in the wake of a promise from God and in anticipation of a future fulfillment of that promise. From the time of Abraham the Hebrews looked forward to the promised land. God fulfilled this promise in the Exodus—the dramatic rescue of his chosen people from slavery in Egypt, the bestowal of the Ten Commandments on Moses, and the entry of the Hebrews into the land of Canaan, flowing with milk and honey. The Israelites looked back upon these events in a special way because in the Exodus was the origin of Israel. God's creation of the Hebrews was celebrated weekly on the Sabbath and annually at Passover. But in contrast to mythical-cyclical cultures they simply remembered the Exodus; they did not reactualize it. "The Exodus event itself can never be repeated," nor can it be made contemporary through religious ritual: "it is frozen in the past."[16]

History arises because God makes promises and fulfills these promises.[17] The people of Israel often found themselves suspended in the tension between promise and fulfillment, and this tension spawned the consciousness that the future can be different from the past. The prophet Nathan promised King David that an anointed king or Messiah would arise from his descendants. This created an atmosphere of anxious expectation during the bloody intrigue and wave of assassinations in his own royal court, and the question was asked: will all David's sons die or will the promise be fulfilled? The promise was kept alive when his son Solomon evaded death and took the throne, and it continued to generate expectant hope on down to the birth of Jesus.

The proclamation of judgment by the prophets deepened the promise-fulfillment scheme and directed attention even more resolutely upon the future. Prophets such as Amos, Ezekiel, and Isaiah looked forward to the Day of the Lord. There would be a day coming in the future, they said, when God would rendezvous with his people. This day would bring a special activity, a special destiny, in which God would destroy the evil powers and safely deliver those who were loyal to him. For Amos the Day of the Lord would be one of calamity; it would be "darkness, and not light." (Amos 5:18) He was announcing that with God things had changed: the old basis for Israel's comfort and salvation was now null and void. The Old Testament scholar Gerhard von Rad labels this characteristic of prophecy "eschatology," because it pronounces a "break . . . so deep that the new state beyond it cannot be understood as the continuation of what went before."[18] In this way, Israel experienced God as one who could and did intervene in the events of history, and such divine intervention brought irreversible changes and new statuses. The anticipation of a future that will be different from the past gives great value to those events which inaugurate that future; the Exodus is remembered for what it is, unique, and unrepeatable.

This has important implications for the freedom of God and the freedom of humanity. The Hebrews believed God was free. He was not tied to the rhythms of nature or cycles of history (just as he was not tied only to the land on which his worshipers resided).[19] Because God could react to human activity on the plane of history by changing his mind, it meant that both God and humans are engaged in a free interplay. To be free means that the decisions and choices I make will significantly determine my destiny in the future. If everything has already been decided in eternity, then my decisions and choices have no consequence. Mythical-cyclical people were not free in this sense; they simply responded to the eternal principles to which even the gods themselves were subject. Without the notion of an open future, in which even God might behave differently than he did in the past, the idea of human freedom could not have been born.

And with freedom came the notion of change as basic. It took the concept of a free god to introduce into Western consciousness the possibility of fundamental change. In the mythical view change is superficial; only the eternal rhythms are real. For the Hebrews, change became ontological.

But there is still a further development we should examine. The fulfillment of God's promises of which the prophets in the Old Testament spoke was believed to be a fulfillment *within* history, *within* the temporal succession of events. With the development of apocalyptic literature and the New Testament, however, God's fulfillment became pictured as coming at the end of history, at the conclusion of time.

The Jewish apocalyptic books mentioned in chapter 2 divide time into two separate and distinct ages or eons. The present eon is the evil age in which Satan's designs control the great processes of history. This eon will come to an end, however, and a new age of righteousness in the kingdom of God will replace it. The old world will be destroyed and there will be a new heaven and a new earth. In the Old Testament view there was great stress on the continuity of events as they moved from promise to fulfillment. Now, there is envisioned a radical and complete change between the old and the new. God's future will end the present.

In the New Testament the Day of the Lord is understood as the parousia, the second coming of Christ. On that day, said Jesus, you " 'will see the Son of man coming in clouds with great power and glory.' " (Mark 13:26) The parousia of Christ will mark the end of time as we know it, the conclusion of human history with the Day of Judgment, the resurrection of the dead, and the advent of the eternal kingdom of God. The crucifixion and resurrection of Jesus were his own personal fate, to be sure, but at the same time these events proleptically anticipate the eschatological future of the world which must pass through judgment and rebirth. Jesus' death and resurrection function for us as a promise that will attain fulfillment in the future when we too will rise from the dead.

What we have here is a vision of the entire scope of human temporality. History begins at creation and proceeds in linear fashion toward a final end and goal supplied by God. We are located somewhere along this temporal continuum with the ability to look back in memory at the promise and forward in expectation of its fulfillment.

In his book *The Theology of Hope* Jürgen Moltmann sums up the implications of the concept of promise for historical time.[20] First, a promise is a declaration that announces the coming of a reality that does not yet exist. This means that the future is open to new things yet to be created by God. Second, the promise binds people to the future and gives them a sense of history. Each event has value in itself because it is not simply a replica of some eternal principle. Third, this history does not consist of cyclic recurrence, but has a definite trajectory towards the promised, yet still outstanding, future fulfillment. The direction is irreversible. Fourth, because of the promise of a new reality to come, our evaluation of the present cannot rest on old means of measurement. If God's fulfillment lies in the future, then the value of the present is gauged by its relationship to that future.

In the modern Western world we are nearly oblivious to the distinctiveness of the dynamic linear concept of time we inherited from Judaism and Christianity. Technological invention, in the sense of consciously creating and manufacturing a new product which appears in human history for the first time, would be impossible without the acceptance of linear time with an open future. And it was from this particular experience of the ancient Hebrews with their God that the foundations for modernity were laid. The notion of the temporal succession of events—of linear time—was always available to other cultures. But, as G. van der Leeuw says, "only in Judaism and Christianity is the idea of the unthinkable, of the beginning and the end, fully thought out."[21]

HOPE AND MEANING

The modern consciousness has accepted the Biblical conception of time as linear and historical, but it has also changed it. The advance of secular thinking has dislodged God from the picture and replaced him with an abstract notion of progress. By losing God we also lose the ground for our hope.

Even though we tend to take the doctrine of progress for granted, Rudolf Bultmann reminds us that "this belief in progress is not in accord with the Christian faith, indeed, it is opposed to it."[22] The notion of progress originated in the polemic arguments against the Christian belief in God's providence, beginning with the eighteenth-century philosopher Voltaire, who believed that humanity was progressing in knowledge and that increased knowledge required a fight against the superstition of the church. The doctrine of progress kept the concept of the advance of time but it jettisoned its faith in God.[23]

When God is removed from the picture, two other elements of historical consciousness are threatened: meaning and hope. The discarding of God threatens to undercut the very notion of progress itself because if God is removed, then there is no extra-human ground for believing in an end to time, so that progress loses its aim and direction. With no aim or direction, it is impossible to determine the meaning of a particular event in the whole scheme of things. We end up with only simple change because we have lost our ability to measure whether a particular development is progressive or not.

In the sacred universe of myth-oriented cultures all events had meaning. Meaning was determined by their relationship to the eternal time depicted in the myth. Myths are ontological, i. e., they portrayed to archaic people the way the world really is because it was created this way by the gods in eternity. So the narrative of how the gods created things back in the time before there was any time was not just a cute story to be told for entertainment. Rather, the behavior of the gods provided paradigms or archetypal models to guide human behavior. Insofar as one imitates the behavior of the gods, one is linked with them in their eternal and sacred reality. In contrast, what people do on their own or disregarding the divine models belongs to the sphere of the profane; hence it is a vain and illusory activity, and, in the last analysis, unreal.[24] For people living in myth-oriented cultures there is a source and criterion of meaning: the ultimate reality provided by the gods. The meaning of temporal events can only be determined by their relationship to the wider context of time, the eternal reality that is their ground.

In the Bible, the ground of meaning and hope is similarly the ground of all reality, namely, God. God is author of both the origin and end of the world. By "end" of the world we mean two things. The first meaning of end is found in the Greek work *terma,* which means end, limit, or boundary. The eschatological end of time is its *terma* because it presents us with the conclusion or *termi*nation of historical movement as we know it. The second meaning of end is found in another Greek word, *telos,* which means end, purpose, or goal. The purpose or goal toward which we are marching provides the context for determining the meaning of individual activities. To speak of God's *telos* for the world is to speak of his will or his law.

It is no mere coincidence that these two meanings converge in the one word "end," however. It is the end in the sense of final destiny or conclusion that provides the ground for speaking of the end as a goal. Without a vision of the final reality the significance or purpose for present activity evaporates. The Greeks and the New Testament writers were already aware of this vital connection, so that the term *telos* was often used to mean termination or cessation as well as purpose or goal.[25] Thus, if meaning and hope are to be more than merely the projected wishes of people, we see that they must be grounded in the one final reality of all things.

Without God's future, the basis for hope in a scheme of linear time is undercut. If we are going to hope that things will progress to a future destiny in which the finest human aspirations will have been achieved, then we need a ground upon which to base that hope. To simply project into the future the things we "wish" would happen and then expect them to occur may lead to illusions and daydreaming. Try as they may to achieve peace on earth, people have never been able to achieve it in the past and have given no convincing signs that they can really do so in the future. If hope is to be realistic and more than mere daydreaming, it must rely upon an extra-human power to fulfill our aspirations.

Without God's future, the basis for meaning in a scheme of linear time evaporates. To understand the meaning of something— and this includes the meaning of one's own life—we must see it in relation to the context of the whole of which it is a part. We do not know the meaning of a word like "run," for instance, unless we know the sentence in which we find it. On one occasion we might say, "the athlete runs in the race," or on another occasion, "the machine runs," while on still another occasion, "the senator will run again for office." And the meaning of the sentence itself may depend on the context of the paragraph in the speech or book where it appears. How often we fault news journalists who quote political figures out of context so that the meaning of what they originally said is distorted. In order to know the meaning of something, you have to know the entire context of which it is a part. This is also true for historical events. To understand the meaning of the French Revolution, historians must examine the cultural and social context of eighteenth-century Europe. Similarly, students of the Bible try to grasp the meaning of what is written there by examining it in the historical context of the Middle East during the time it was being written. However, the meaning of an event is not determined only by its past context, but by its future as well. The context of meaning for the Constitution of the United States written in 1787 includes many events that followed it: additional amendments, Supreme Court decisions, impeachment trials, the Civil War, etc. And the full meaning of the Constitution cannot yet be determined because it will continue to be interpreted and to influence us in the future.

Events have their meaning in the cultural or personal life-setting in which they occur, and the meaning of this life-setting is similarly subject to the context of the larger epoch in world history to which it belongs. And each epoch in turn requires for its meaning the most comprehensive context, namely, the whole of world history itself.[26] The full meaning of an event can be seen only in light of the whole reality of which it is a part; any smaller context of interpretation will leave meaning fragmentary and dubious.

The meaning of any decision in the present, then, is determined by its effect on future actualities. And its ultimate meaning is finally dependent on the whole of human history. Without at least a preliminary vision of this whole we can only wonder whether or not our decisions and and actions can have any real significance.

The Biblical picture of God's history from creation to eschaton provided in at least an anticipatory way a vision of the whole, wherein the purpose and meaning of things could be ascertained. With the removal of God from the scheme in modern times, however, the future has been left so wide open—with neither *terma* nor *telos*—that any notion of the whole has disappeared. Because the future has become increasingly an unknown, we can no longer interpret our present activity with confidence. The appearance in the twentieth century of Existentialist nihilism in the writings of people like Sartre and Camus reflects our sense of the loss of meaning.

Hope for progress in the future depends upon faith in God, and this is the source of meaning in life. Without God progress degenerates into mere purposeless change and the realistic person admits that there is no other extra-human ground on which we can base a hope. The Dutch sociologist Fred L. Polak senses this evisceration of the secular ethos of progress:

> Thus, in the development of Western civilization we have seen man shift from a passive drift toward a future Kingdom of Heaven to a sudden seizing of the rudder with full mastery of the arts of navigation. His increasing skills in agriculture and medicine gave him a new power over life and death. Now, unexpectedly, the hand on the rudder wavers. Man continues to try to steer, but apathy has overcome him, and life seems to be an "existence to the death." Was the faith in human power but a bubble, to be pricked so soon?[27]

Forecasters of unprecedented population growth and worldwide starvation assume that time is one-directional. There is no return to a mythical past. We are going only one place: to the future we will create.

Our bookstands have been inundated recently with numerous volumes on the future that we may classify as doomsday books. The most recent and finest so far is the one mentioned earlier authored by Robert L. Heilbroner, *An Inquiry into the Human Prospect.* The first paragraph of the book opens with the question, "Is there hope for man?" Heilbroner seeks to be as realistic and objective as possible about the present trends of world population growth, environmental destruction, and war. After concluding his analysis he reflects on the human prospect: "If then, by the question 'Is there hope for man?' we ask whether it is possible to meet the challenges of the future without the payment of a fearful price, the answer must be: No, there is no such hope."[28] People living in myth-oriented or Bible-oriented cultures could have hope because they knew that the future was grasped securely by the divine ground of reality. Modern people have inherited the consciousness of linear time born out of the Hebrew experience with God, but now that they have pushed God out of the picture, they are left only with the terror of the history they themselves must produce.

6
VALUES
FOR A PLANETARY SOCIETY

Congruent with the notion of linear time, yet somewhat incongruent with the feeling that we are being overwhelmed by forces of change that are beyond human control, is the assumption of modern science that we can and will produce the future we desire if we make the appropriate decisions. Another characteristic of our modern future consciousness is the demand for understanding, decision, and control. It is believed that if we can understand the forces that presently govern the course of events, and if we decide to take the proper actions, we will then gain control of our own destiny and guide our world into a truly "human" future.

Alvin Toffler states the challenge succinctly in the introduction to his book *The Futurists:* ". . . if we do not change the future, we shall be compelled to endure it."[1] And what do we need to make it possible for us to change the future? The answer most often given is understanding. Toffler says that "diagnosis precedes cure" and that we must "understand in greater detail how the effects of acceleration penetrate . . . personal life."[2] Charles Reich says the same thing: "What we do not understand, we cannot control."[3] The formula seems to be:

lack of understanding = powerlessness
understanding + decision = control

The thesis is that understanding somehow elevates people above fate and places them in the driver's seat.

This feeling that we are "the masters of our fate and the captains of our soul" seems to persist in our future consciousness right along with the opposite feeling of impotency in the face of overwhelming change. However, if it were not for some confidence in our power to determine our own fate the intense moral tone in future consciousness would evaporate. Our experience of the openness of our future—that it can be either good or bad—combines with confidence in our own capacities, producing a sense of moral responsibility. This sense of moral responsibility is inescapably a part of future consciousness.

Futurology takes us down a blind alley, though. We are told we must make a decision, but we are not told which decision is the right one. Moral criteria, which we could use to orient and evaluate our decisions, cannot honestly be provided by scientific futurology. Yet the pressure to make decisions is intense.

This is the rub. What does it mean to make something happen for the good? Science can impress upon us our responsibility for making decisions, but it cannot tell us which decisions to make. We need a vision of what the ultimate good of humanity is in order to rank our priorities and decide how to plan our future. But due to the pervasiveness of the cultural malaise described by Robert Heilbroner earlier, we seem to have lost our center of value and orientation. Consequently, we are tempted to avoid making decisions and simply to let the juggernaut of technology roll on with no one at the helm. We can choose to regain control over the dynamics of change and make technology serve human ends and purposes, or we can choose to allow technology to wind its own way through history while we simply oil its gears. Either way, our destiny is our own responsibility.

As the pressure mounts to make decisions and plans, we see that the futurists themselves already have an implicit image of what our destiny should be: it ought to be a future in which we live in harmony with nature, the rich share with the poor, and all of us share a single planet-wide brotherhood. Futurists cannot really do their work without at least a disguised vision of their ultimate concern for humanity's destiny. This implicit vision must be made explicit so that it can more greatly affect the decisions we make.

We are flat on our backs screaming about the need for making the right decisions because we feel too impotent to do so. What we need is an explicit vision of ultimate human destiny that so tantalizes our imaginations and fires up our confidence that deciding and planning for a truly human future becomes an exciting challenge rather than an aversive chore. Hope in the coming kingdom of God can do that.

TRADE-OFFS FOR AN ECO-HUMAN FUTURE

The Club of Rome begins their analysis of the future of our planet's ecosphere and its people by saying that our basic problem is our lack of understanding of how the world system works. "The predicament of mankind," as they call it, is that we do "not understand the origins, significance, and inter-relationships of its many components and thus [are] . . . unable to devise effective responses."[4] If they mean just what they say—that our problem is one of *understanding* of the world system—then the publication and reading of *The Limits to Growth* by the masses would itself resolve the predicament, because this book does present a clear understanding. I contend that ours is more than merely a problem in understanding; and even the Club of Rome emphasizes the need— beyond understanding—for decision and control. "As soon as a society recognizes that it cannot maximize everything for everyone, it must begin to make choices."[5]

The Club's goal is to alert us to the finite limits of growth on earth, but at the same time they point out that people have demonstrated that they do not necessarily "learn" from understanding those limits. The Club presents the whaling industry as a case in point. Whalers have reached one limit after another and have attempted to overcome each one by simply employing more technology. As a result, they have wiped out one species after another. First, the industry began by killing off the biggest whales, the blues. Then in the 1940s, when the stock of blue whales was giving out, they switched to killing fin whales. In the 1960s they had to turn to sei whales, and now the sperm whale is being hunted without any limit on numbers. Because of the increasing scarcity of whales, among other factors, the whalers have increased the tonnage and horsepower of catcher boats. But their efficiency has plummeted; the average production of whale oil per catcher boat per day's work has fallen to 30% of what it was in 1960. The outcome of

this grow-forever policy of the whaling industry can only be the final
extinction of both whales and whalers. The alternative policy, of
course, would be to impose a *limit* on the number of whales taken
each year, set so that the whale population is maintained at a
steady-state level. This self-imposed limit on whaling would be an
unpleasant pressure that would prevent the further growth of the
industry, but perhaps it would be preferable to the gradual disappearance of whales and the ultimate collapse of the whaling industry.

It is this basic choice between alternative futures that the whole
planet is facing in every department. Is it better to try to live within
a natural limit by accepting a self-imposed restriction on growth? Or
is it preferable to press on toward that natural limit, risking disaster,
in the hope that some unforeseen technological innovation will
sweep that limit away? The problem is enhanced by the fact that
our "whole culture has evolved around the principle of fighting
against limits rather than learning to live with them."[6]

These choices are aptly called "trade-offs." We cannot have
both inexpensive industrial processing and an unpolluted ecosphere;
we must trade off one for the other. In order to guarantee the
availability of unrenewable natural resources in the future, policies
must be adopted now that will decrease resource use in the present.
Should there be more people or more wealth? more wilderness or
more automobiles? more food for the poor or more services for the
rich? In short, we cannot both eat our cake and have it too. And
it is time for deciding which we are going to do.[7]

Rationally chosen trade-offs now can defuse the population
timebomb, says Lester R. Brown, economist and senior fellow at the
Overseas Development Council in Washington, D. C.[8] He believes
that if we trade off our relentless demand for superaffluence and our
traditional policies and programs surrounding child production, then
we will gain the ability to stabilize the world population at six billion
by the year 2015. To achieve this the peoples of the world must
make decisions in three areas.

First, decisions must be aimed at international economic policies
which will help the poorer countries develop the necessary social
conditions for human fertility decline. As we saw above, populations

are growing much more slowly in the more developed countries—
there is a positive correlation between affluence and low fertility—
and Mr. Brown believes stability here could be achieved as early
as 1985. In the less developed countries, however, not only are
birth rates far in excess of death rates, but there is a disproportion-
ately high percentage of women presently at the childbearing age.
The final step to world population equilibrium could still be taken
by 2015 if sufficient attention could be given to designing the
economic and social policies that produce the fundamental improve-
ments in material well-being that bring decreased fertility. A major
increase in the general flow of resources from rich countries to poor
is urgently needed, in conjunction with domestic policies that will
enlist average citizens in participating fully in their nation's development. We must begin by launching major programs to weld an
international food reserve system, to expand fertilizer and food
production for the small farmers in the underdeveloped sector of the
world, to make health care universal, and to provide education to
the level of literacy for all adults.

These international programs alone will not solve the problem
completely; they point us to the second matrix of decisions: the
domestic policies of the developing nations. More jobs, better
health, education, and economic security must become available to
the people. Economic Incentives are important. Government policies
such as income-tax deductions, maternity and child-care subsidies,
social security provisions, etc., should be constructed to provide an
incentive to keep family size small. The object must be to offer, on
the one hand, positive inducements for limiting family size and, on
the other, measures to discourage large families. In addition to
general economic incentives, we need policies that will open up
more career options for women. In some societies a combination
of law and custom restricts a woman's right to work, to own property, to vote, to hold political office, and to pursue traditionally
"male" professions. What else is there for her to do but have
children? Eliminating these restrictive laws and customs would help
divert women's attention away from maternity, as it has clearly done
in the affluent West.

The third matrix of decisions has to do with family-planning programs. The United Nations Fund for Population Activities (UNFPA) estimates that the cost of providing family-planning services ranges from fifty cents to one dollar per year per person. Excluding China, the less developed countries contain approximately two billion people. On the basis of the UNFPA estimate of one dollar per person, it would require two billion dollars to provide family-planning services throughout those countries. Lester Brown suggests that this expense be divided in two, half coming from international sources and the other half from governmental or private sources within each country involved.

These are the decisions students of population growth are placing on the doorstep of the peoples of the world. It is a question of survival for all; but once we understand the implications of the problem, we will be able to decide in favor of the actions necessary to resolve it. Brown believes that "If population growth is permitted to continue unchecked, the prospect is desperate. But if the complexity of the problem is recognized, and the right combination of measures launched even at this late hour, the outlook is not hopeless. A rational and humane solution to the population problem, while not simple, is well within our capability."[9] The proper understanding of things, accompanied by decisions to make rational trade-offs, will give us control over our own future.

What do the trade-off recommendations by the Club of Rome and Lester Brown reveal? First, they seem to include the assumption that humanity is a single whole, within which the parts are interdependent, and that our concerns should be directed towards the survival and edification of all people. Second, this implies that selfishness is wrong because it leads not only to the destruction of nature and the forsaking of some human beings, but eventually it leads to self-destruction.

Although technically unable to provide a value system according to which we are supposed to make our decisions, these futurists presuppose a complete vision of what people are and what they ought to decide to become. This implicit vision of the future that we can make for ourselves roughly corresponds to the more abstract but quite explicit vision of the eschatological kingdom of God. And the scope and the importance of the choices we are being asked to confront are entering the realm of ultimacy at least insofar as they concern all humanity rather than just a selfish few.

TOWARD A PLANETARY SOCIETY

The choice is becoming one between survival for all or survival for none, a choice between utopia and oblivion. The world is rapidly becoming a single planetary society, for good or ill. Our young people have been reared by the third parent—television—which has given them hourly news of world events. Unlike any previous generations, our youth think "world." The communication advances of the electronic media have shrunk the entire world into a "global village." Through electricity we can know instantly what happens on the other side of the globe. Marshall McLuhan argues that the electronic media have become extensions of the individual's nervous system. "We have extended our central nervous system itself in a global embrace, abolishing both space and time as far as our planet is concerned."[10] Increasingly, we share the thoughts and feelings of the rest of humanity. There is virtually no escape from the media.

And electronic communication is always accompanied by its big brother, economic interdependence. Modern industry and international trade work only as part of a single world system. For example, the very important steel-making constituent manganese is found plentifully in Ghana, but it is useless to Ghanaians because they have neither iron nor coal with which to make steel. Instead Ghanaian manganese must be transported overseas to be made into steel, which will then be exported back to Ghana and other countries as tools, machinery, and structural components. International trade is taking mined resources from all around the world and transporting them to a few points of maximum industrial efficiency, and then redistributing them as manufactured goods. Even the trees in the United States are being cut in order to make packing crates in which the Japanese send Americans television sets. R. Buckminster Fuller says, "industrialization is inherently world-embracing and world-integrating."[11]

And with the rise of multi-national corporations in the twentieth century the economic ties between the world's peoples are even negating the boundaries set by the political leaders of nation-states. Today there are about three hundred of these colossal multi-nationals, whose combined production of goods and services adds up to about $300 billion per year. No country in the world other than the United States has a larger gross national product. General Motors alone, the largest multi-national, has total annual sales of $25 billion, which exceeds the net national income of all but a dozen countries. It is not so much their size that should be stressed here, but rather their influence in linking together the scattered parts of the world. The move from the industrial to the post-industrial era in the developed countries is being accompanied by a move from the pre-industrial to the industrial era in the rest of the world. This is being aided in part by the action of multi-nationals who are transferring manufacturing production to the low-wage countries. In the first five years of the 1970s, for example, overall employment in electronics in the United States declined by some 219,000 jobs as American firms relocated plants in Singapore, Hong Kong, Taiwan, and Mexico. More and more manufacturing of the standardized sort will move to the poorer parts of the world, while the more affluent societies will concentrate on management, information processing, and research and development. For good or ill the control of the interchange will remain in the hands of the multi-national corporation, but the system of economic interdependence uniting the various races and classes of the world's peoples is increasing.

Leftists are quick to criticize multi-national corporations because they appear to sponsor American economic and cultural imperialism. Multi-nationals deserve criticism, to be sure, but it should be pointed out that they are not distinctively American. Many originated in the United States, of course, but many others originated in other countries. Philips, Shell, Unilever, Nestlé, Volkswagen exploit supranational operations just as vigorously as any American firm. Harvard economist John Kenneth Galbraith argues that the technostructures of all multi-national corporations evolve from the same basic need to lower production costs and protect price stability. This is true regardless of national origin. The reason the hotels, automobiles, service stations, office equipment, and airline operations purveyed by multi-national corporations are all much the same is not because they are American but because they are all products of the same kind of executive technostructure.[12] The world is approaching unity not through American cultural imperialism but through the not-so-subtle expansion of a particular way of doing business.

The role of the multi-nationals in drawing the peoples of the world toward a single planetary society deserves further comment. The typical liberationist criticism that such corporations are dehumanizing simply because they are "big" misses the mark. One of the false presuppositions on the basis of which most critics of modern society do their thinking is the assumption that the essence of human life and culture is economic. Economics has become the all-embracing category within which questions regarding the meaning of human existence are discussed. Marx's doctrine of economic determinism seems to have been fully imbibed.

But this leads to a contradiction. After assuming that extra-human or non-human forces such as economic structures are all-determining, the critics then complain that our economic structures are dehumanizing. The remedial action recommended consists simply of manipulating the economic structures to make life more human; it does not consist of a transformation in the human heart. Somehow this change in the non-human is supposed to humanize.

This leads to countless inconsistencies that have gone virtually unnoticed among the rhetoricians of contemporary futurism. We are asked to embrace global holism but are then told that global business—the multi-national corporation—is taboo. We are enjoined to break up such organizations into smaller businesses with local worker control. Local worker control is said to be more personalized, therefore more human. We are asked to recognize global interdependence and at the same time to strive for local autonomy. Would not common sense require that we either fish or cut bait?[13]

I believe the problem in this thinking is the erroneous assumption that we can personalize or humanize our daily life by changing the structures of our institutions. This assumption fails to recognize that the recent widespread use of this term "structures" came into vogue for the express purpose of pointing to the non-human or impersonal elements of institutional life. During the civil rights activities of the 1960s, for example, people who claimed to be personally unprejudiced toward blacks justified their overt practices of racial discrimination by blaming the structures of the system. Instead of blaming individuals for our social evils we began passing the guilt off on to structures and systems. This practice eased the white liberal conscience because it permitted the finger of guilt to point anywhere except toward one's own heart. If the challenges posed by future consciousness are to be met, they will be met only through moral decision-making, and moral decisions are always made by people and never by structures.

A conversation that consumer advocate Ralph Nader says took place between him and the president of the Coca Cola Company will illustrate my point. The distribution success of Coca Cola's marketing executives is nothing short of phenomenal. There is almost no place on our planet that does not have Coke on sale. Coca Cola was selling in the Soviet Union during the deepest freezes of the Cold War in the Eisenhower years. In Upper Volta during drought one can buy a Coke. Here is a company that has covered the globe more thoroughly than the United Nations. What a potential factor in behalf of world unity this communications network could provide!

Mr. Nader pointed out that Coca Cola has no nourishing value whatsoever. He asked the company's president if they would consider slipping a few vitamins into the drink. The huge distribution capabilities at the command of this business could thus be pressed into the service of the war against world hunger.

The Coca Cola executive said he was sorry but such a measure could not be considered even with the guarantee that the vitamins would not change the drink's taste. Why? Because his company had only one purpose: to earn money by selling a "refreshing" drink. Even though he personally sympathized with the plight of the world's malnourished peoples, his professional responsibilities were to the corporation's board and stockholders.

What we have here is clearly a values conflict. Values are human; they are not structured into our institutions. Ralph Nader could see the potential power of the Coca Cola institution in the war against hunger. The Coca Cola executives are able to see this same potential but they make their decisions according to different priorities. And it is they—not Nader—who are in control of the institution.

What should Ralph Nader do? Work to destroy Coca Cola International by advocating smaller soft-drink bottling and distribution companies? Should he advocate local worker control? Would that feed the hungry and manourished peoples of Upper Volta? Of course not. There are other multi-nationals of a slightly different type who operate with different values and priorities. They are CARE, the World Council of Churches, the Lutheran World Federation, the Roman Catholic Church, and others. These multi-nationals are certainly more modest in size and influence than General Motors or Coca Cola. But they have been working relentlessly with their structures to feed the poor and aid the malnourished all through the crisis of the early 1970s. It is just the qualities of bigness and internationality that made these communications networks so appropriate for sharing on a worldwide scale. To break them up in favor of local control because local control is ostensibly more human would undermine their global effectiveness.

The problem with multi-national businesses is not structural; it is a value problem. Had ITT, Exxon, Shell, GM, and Coca Cola allied themselves with the charitable organizations, perhaps millions of lives would have been saved from starvation during the 1973–75 period. But doing business as usual held a higher priority for them. This is a human issue and the responsibility for it cannot be simply shifted to the shoulders of an amorphous doctrine of determinism by impersonal economic structures. The breakup of multi-nationals will not automatically foster a deeply spiritual sense of world community, and it may even rid us of strategic global communications networks. Our multi-nationals need a new goal orientation, not a breakup.

§

Another area which is drawing the various peoples of the world into a single community because important decisions are pressing is energy. We are running out of our conventional supplies. We are extremely dependent upon petroleum and the planet's reserves are dwindling rapidly. By the year 2000 oil production in the non-Communist world is expected to fall short of meeting demand by 15 million to 20 million barrels per day. And this estimate presumes that coal production will double, that the output of nuclear-generated power multiplies 15 times, and that conservation measures cut the increase in petroleum demand to half its historic growth rate. We knew it could not last forever. A remedy is needed, and whatever remedy is proposed will have implications that are worldwide in scope.

With the skyrocketing price of oil, the limited supplies of petroleum and natural gas, the pollution hazards of coal burning and nuclear fission, scientists have begun looking for a new concept in energy. The most promising source of energy for the future is nuclear fusion. The fusion process is that employed in the explosion of the great H-bombs. The fuel for nuclear fusion is deuterium which is found abundantly in water; one gallon of sea water can deliver energy equal to three hundred gallons of gasoline. But to develop fusion we will need planet-wide cooperation.

There are three chief reasons why nuclear fusion holds promise for the future. First, it does not pollute. The fusion process does not result in radioactive ashes and produces minimal radiation. It is far less dangerous than the nuclear fission presently in use; fission creates a large amount of dangerous radioactive wastes. Second, in a time when the reserves of conventional energy sources are dwindling—fossil fuel will last less than 150 years—fusion fuel is virtually inexhaustible. The total deuterium reserve in the ocean waters is good for billions of years at any conceivable rate of use. Third, fusion energy resists being diverted for purposes of war. Fission reactors use substances which can be converted into nuclear weapons. Fusion reactors do not. Fission reactors could be sabotaged with disastrous environmental consequences. Fusion reactors could not.

Controlled nuclear fusion is possible sometime beyond 1980, but research and development will be extremely costly. Trade-offs will have to be made for it. It will have to be a multi-billion dollar development program, which no one company—not even General Motors—could undertake. Perhaps it is even too big for one nation. Everyone will have to cooperate in laboring for its birth. The physicist Richard Post says there is no real reason why nations should not share their know-how. It is just as much in the interest of the United

States for Chile to have inexpensive energy as it is for the U. S. to have it. The primary fuel, deuterium, is available to everyone. The energy situation requires cooperation on a new scale; fusion could give energy to everyone on our planet and make competition for it a thing of the past. Post believes this could be "the most revolutionary thing that has happened in a thousand years."[14]

And even pollution is drawing the world into a single planetary society, as the entire world shares the same dangers. We cannot protect ourselves against other people's contaminants. If a toxic substance were to be introduced into a room full of people, everyone in it would succumb together. So also with the world. We all share the same ecosphere, so the danger that faces it is shared by everyone.

Pollution itself could provide an opportunity to bring the peoples of the world together for more positive purposes. It might not, however. Right now the problem of pollution has not yet been solved, and we should worry that as soon as a partial technological solution is discovered it might be used to box off part of the world, condemning some people to disaster and preserving only a few. Margaret Mead, the famous anthropologist, is campaigning to deepen and broaden the feeling of brotherhood for all humanity so that the decisions we make regarding pollution will accrue to everyone's benefit and not merely to that of the privileged few.[15]

We are becoming a single planetary society whether we like it or not; and if we are to survive, the values that presently direct our economic institutions must change to embrace this planetary perspective. Systems theorist Ervin Laszlo says that "the values of the large majority of the human population need to be shifted from parochial and national orientation to the global perspective."[16] Economist Kenneth Boulding argues that we will have to decide to abandon our present "cowboy" mentality and begin to think of the earth as a spaceship. Boulding associates our present open economy with the cowboy's reckless, exploitive, romantic, and violent behavior, which is permitted because the cowboy lives on the wide open, illimitable plains. But as the world becomes one and we recognize our interdependence one with another all over the globe, we must begin to view ours as a closed economy and plan accordingly. Our earth is like a spaceship sent on a mission with a finite number of supplies for the crew to consume. The earth does not make available unlimited reservoirs of everything for our extraction and pollution. "Therefore, man must find his place in a cyclical ecological system which is capable of continuous reproduction of material form even though it cannot escape having inputs of energy."[17]

As we enter the era of the planetary society, breakdowns in one part of the world-system will eventually cause a breakdown in every other part. Survival must be for all or none. We can no longer afford poverty in the world. We can no longer afford ignorance or prejudice that leads to neglect. All children need a share in the world's abundance—good health and an education—not only to develop their own God-given potentialities but also to be able to maximize the value of what they can share with the rest of the world. When President Eisenhower was confronted by the information on the projected damage of a nuclear war, he said, "There is no alternative to peace." John Platt restates it a bit more precisely, "The world has now become too dangerous for anything less than Utopia."[18]

Humanity is now thought to be taking control of its evolutionary progress, and the decisions we make are of paramount importance. We have begun to see the possibility of reshaping the human organism, as we have been reshaping plant and animal organisms for many years, into new forms that may eventually lead to the use of the full creative potentialities of the protoplasm in the human brain. The human race may cease to be at the mercy of the evolutionary accidents that produced its physical frame and its society. Through conscious decisions we may be able to remake ourselves both biologically and socially.

But as we approach the limits to growth, there is considerable pressure mounting to make appropriate decisions now. John Platt points out that in the past we have existed as isolated human beings, selfish, combative, ignorant, helpless. But over the last few centuries "the great evolutionary hormones of knowledge and technology have been pressing us . . . into power and prosperity and communication and interaction, and into increasing tolerance and vision and choice and planning—pressing us, whether we like it or not, into a single coordinated humankind."[19] Platt sees people and nations everywhere beginning to deliberately design their development with a growing confidence in their power to choose their own future. Platt is a firm believer in the understanding-decision-control formula. He says that "if we are wise and energetic and understand our own nature and purposes well enough to restructure and control these dangers [exponential growth], mankind may emerge very quickly into coordinated forms such as it has never known before. . . . We have been men. We are emerging into Man."[20] Although he is an optimist with regard to human capabilities, Platt still recognizes that the human race may not survive the next few years. He compares our present situation with that of a rocket on a launching pad. We have been preparing for this moment of takeoff for a long time, and if we can manage to get safely through the takeoff period, we may fly on a new and exciting course for a long time to come. But at this moment, as the powerful new engines are fired, their thrust and roar shake and stress every part of the ship and may cause the whole project to blow up before we can steer it on its way. Our task today is to harness and direct our newfound powers toward the new world instead of toward destruction. Unless we can do this, the rapidly increasing strains and crises of the next decades may kill us all.[21] Buckminster Fuller states it this way: "Success or failure is now all of humanity's responsibility."[22]

It is a choice between utopia or oblivion, but many futurists are confident that it is a choice we can make and a destiny we ourselves can determine. John Platt reiterates his faith in our ability to save ourselves:

> We will move, if we survive the strain, to a wealthy and powerful and coordinated world society reaching across the solar system, a society that might find out how to keep itself alive and evolving for thousands or millions or billions of years, a time as long as all of evolution past. It is a tremendous prospect. Hardly anyone has seen the enormous sweep and restructuring and unity and future of it except perhaps dreamers like H. G. Wells or Teilhard de Chardin. It is a quantum jump. It is a new state of matter. The act of saving ourselves, if it

succeeds, will make us participants in the most incredible
event in evolution. It is the step to Man.[23]

Certainly this vision of a future utopia is glorious, and certainly
humans must take responsibility for decision-making. But the eschatological problem arises here again; how can alienated people
through a decision of their own will produce a de-alienated society?
Or in the words of more traditional theology: on what basis can we
expect a sinful humanity to suddenly choose sharing over selfishness,
cooperation over competition, wisdom over ignorance, and unity
over division, simply because threatened with destruction? Such a
threat has not worked in the past.

And the idea of human sin is not merely the promulgation of
some church doctrine! It is part of the reality we face every day
when we picture to ourselves the future that humans need to have.
The Club of Rome, Lester Brown, Buckminster Fuller, Victor Ferkiss,
John Platt, and Robert Heilbroner all emphasize the necessity for the
human race to decide to make the trade-offs necessary for its
survival. The present generation needs to make sacrifices so that our
children's children might have a chance. We need to feel with future
human beings a bond of such strength that we will sacrifice some
of our present affluence and nationalistic fervor on behalf of our
progeny's future survival. But if we cannot expect a leopard to
change its spots, how can we expect such a radical change in
people and their values? Heilbroner raises the question: "When
men can generally acquiesce in, even relish, the destruction of their
living contemporaries, when they can regard with indifference or
irritation the fate of those who live in slums, rot in prison, or starve
in lands that have meaning only insofar as they are vacation resorts,
why should they be expected to take the painful actions needed to
prevent the destruction of future generations whose faces they will
never live to see?"[24] And Heilbroner provokes a chilling fear when
he writes, "we face the horrendous possibility that humanity may
react to the approach of environmental danger by indulging in a vast
fling while it is still possible—a fling entirely justified by the estima-
tion of present enjoyments over future ones."[25]

People are clearly the problem because although they have the potential for reorienting their values to resolve the dangers, they do not take the opportunity to do so. Heilbroner is a social researcher and not a theologian, but he has certainly portrayed the human dilemma that religious people of times past once referred to as sin. God's grace used to be trusted as the remedy for sin, and this provided the person of faith with hope. Heilbroner counts on no grace, only human decision, so for him there is no hope.

THE VALUE VACUUM

The futurists tell us that the kind of future we will have is in our own hands; it is up to us to make the appropriate decisions and commitments. But what are the appropriate decisions and commitments? In order to make decisions we must have priorities. We must have a criterion for discerning what is important and valuable in order to choose from among the alternatives the futurists lay out for us. Daniel Bell says, "*the* problem of the future consists in defining one's priorities and making the necessary commitments."[26] The question the theologian will want carefully posed is, "Where will the priorities come from?"

Our priorities derive from the things we value, from the things that concern us most. Valuing is a form of taking an interest in something; anything I consciously want is a value for me. A priority is something that has higher value or commands more concern than something else; that is why it comes "prior." The concept of priorities indicates that values come in systems or structures, in which various concerns are ranked according to relative priority. This implies that in each system there is a basic value of ultimate concern, a *summum bonum* or highest good, according to which the relative value of subordinate priorities is determined.

It is also clear that valuing is relevant to all aspects of a person. We value existentially, that is, as whole persons. No aspect of ourselves is left untouched. The ultimate concern of our life forms a kind of center, around which, consciously or unconsciously, our personality is oriented.

Similarly, the ultimate concern and resulting system of priorities held in common by members of a society function to integrate those members into a single culture. The value system and shared concerns of a people are the source of cultural integration and inspiration for committed action. What the culture of our emerging planetary society needs now is an affirmative vision of the future with such drawing power that it becomes the center of our value system, integrates us around a single purpose, and thereby helps us to establish the priorities needed for our present decision-making.

The problems we face as we confront the future cannot be eliminated with technical solutions. A technical solution may be defined as "one that requires a change only in the techniques of the natural sciences, demanding little or nothing in the way of change in human values or ideas of morality."[27] What to do about the nuclear arms race or racial hatred is not merely a technical problem. Do we want to compensate blacks or women for past deprivations by giving them jobs and medical school admissions regardless of their qualifications to compete with white males for the same positions? Do we want to keep a redwood forest, or provide a lucrative industry for a local community? Should a new highway go through an older section of the community, or do we preserve that part of town by re-routing the highway at a greater expense to all? Do we build a nuclear fission power plant and risk radioactive pollution and eventual political terrorism, or do we take the more difficult but safer route of burning our large supply of coal? These issues, and thousands more, cannot be settled on the basis of technical criteria alone. They necessarily involve human values and the priorities according to which moral and political choices are made.[28]

The ground or source for the value system that establishes these priorities is becoming increasingly difficult to locate. Values are changing. Herman Kahn perceives a trend toward the erosion of the work-oriented, achievement-oriented, advancement-oriented values, and a growth toward sensate, secular, humanistic, perhaps self-indulgent criteria for determining what is good.[29] At present we have both sets of values side by side in an unhappy marriage, or better, in a generation squabble.

In the bourgeois-industrial society the "life-style" of the social structure was shaped by the linear sense of progress and the calculation of work and time. People's fundamental efforts were directed towards mastering nature through technology in order to free linear time from the seasonal rhythms of life that bound people to the soil. The projected goal of technical mastery accepted the idea of delayed gratification; in contrast to the child throwing a tantrum, maturity was defined as one's ability to postpone short-term pleasures in order to achieve long-range goals. "Save your money for a rainy day" meant the accumulation of capital and, thereby, an almost indefinite postponement of the rainy day. Along with the virtues of thrift and frugality, dedication to the job, hard work, sobriety, and honesty were seen as services to God, as proof of one's self-worth, and as grounds for social respectability. To a large extent, bourgeois society of the nineteenth century was an integrated whole in which culture, character structure, and economy were infused with a single value system. This was the civilization of capitalism at its apogee.

But, ironically, capitalism itself sowed the seeds that led to the undermining of its own value structure. Mass production led to mass consumption, which destroyed the Protestant ethic by promoting a hedonistic way of life. Hedonism is the doctrine that pleasure is the sole good, and by the middle of the twentieth century, capitalism sought to justify itself not through work as fulfillment but through the promotion of pleasure. The rising standard of living and the relaxation of morals became ends in themselves.

Paradoxically, both value systems are still with us. In the organization of commerce and industry, the system demands thrift in planning, industriousness, self-control, and dedication to a career and success. In the realm of consumption, on the other hand, the reigning values are extravagance and display, freedom from tradition and moral constraint, a fascination with the aberrant, and the compulsive search for play. The two systems are contradictory. Like two male cats in a burlap bag, they are struggling both against each other and against the bag. No longer do we have a culture with an integrated set of values which can provide the ranking of priorities needed for decision-making. In both realms the system is completely mundane, for any transcendent ethic has vanished.

In the struggle, Daniel Bell is convinced that hedonism is winning and although the value system of capitalism repeats the old pieties, they ring hollow to the ears of the new life-style. One characteristic of the new mood in particular will continue to inhibit the growth of an integrated value system; it is the new antinomianism. The term "antinomian," coming from *anti* (against) and *nomos* (law, rule), was originally a theological word referring to the belief that a saved Christian was no longer subject to God's law. Bell uses it in reference to the secular moral order and the radical individualism that flails against traditions and institutions that try to make the individual part of a larger whole. The antinomian attitude is the radical "I" (Ferkiss's liberal individual) asserting its own omnipotence, assuming its own ultimacy, denying its own finite creaturehood, idolatrously seeking to become self-infinitizing through the ecstatic denial of the reality of death. Liberal modernism expressed the antinomian attitude first through art, with its break with the rational cosmology of ordered time and space, of sequence and proportion, of foreground and background, of distance and control, which had been the aesthetic modes of organizing experience for the previous four centuries. In addition to modernism, the revolution of life-style in the counterculture sanctions the acting-out impulse, emigration to a world of fantasy, extreme experiences, and sexual license all under a creed of personal freedom. The antinomianism of our emerging post-industrial society is not only a devolution from higher ideals in the past; more significantly for our discussion here, it is totally unequipped to guide our civilization in its decision-making for the future. The real error of this desire to transgress all laws, limits, and taboos is the implicit belief that when people deny their condition as creatures, they can become gods. This pride, the Club of Rome has demonstrated, may itself lead us to a premature limit that we cannot overcome on our own. Bell says that

> a technocratic society is not ennobling. Material goods provide only transient satisfaction or an invidious superiority over those with less. Yet one of the deepest human impulses is to *sanctify* their institutions and beliefs in order to find a meaningful purpose in their lives and to deny the meaninglessness of death. A post-industrial society cannot provide a transcendent ethic—except for the few who devote themselves to the temple of

science. And the antinomian attitude plunges one into a radical autism which, in the end, dirempts the cords of community and the sharing with others. The lack of a rooted moral belief system is the cultural contradiction of the society, the deepest challenge to its survival.[30]

Bell states the problem well, but he offers no direction or solution. Victor Ferkiss does. He agrees with Bell that there is no central value structure that serves to integrate cultural institutions; there is no widely accepted set of priorities for deciding what to do with our technology.[31] In contrast to Bell, however, he attributes our "sensate, materialistic, individualistic attitude" to the era of the liberal, to the bourgeois-industrial era from which we have just come, and not to the post-industrial technological period which we are entering.[32] In fact, Ferkiss fears that the old values, especially the exploitation of nature and competition for wealth, will persist into the new era of technology and be more destructive than constructive. "Technological man" has not yet emerged. Ferkiss believes that industrial society is not so much being transformed into a post-industrial technological society as it is breaking down— economically, politically, and culturally.[33] He feels that we must break the chains of the industrial era in order to free us to give birth to "technological man."

Ferkiss says that "technological man" will control technology and direct it toward human ends. But what are those ends? From what does the value system come? In his earlier book, *Technological Man,* he says, "Technological man, by definition, will be possessed of the world-view of science and technology, which will themselves provide a standard of value for future civilization."[34] Two things can be said about this statement. The first is to note that "technological man" is said to be grounded in a value system "by definition." Ferkiss has already admitted that "technological man" does not exist and, if the human race decides to destroy itself, may never even come into being at all. So "the standard of value for future civilization" which comes to us by way of "definition" is finally the product of a utopian dream by Victor Ferkiss. It does not have claim to a transcendent basis any more substantial than Ferkiss's own imagination.

But that is not all. Ferkiss is also saying that this "standard of value" emerges essentially from "the world-view of science and technology." This might be satisfactory in one sense: if it is the task of science and technology to apprehend the world—to understand reality—then we would have a standard of value based in reality itself, and that is a form of solid ground. Many a fine ethical system in the past has based the "ought" on what "is." Ferkiss has already prevented himself from taking this route, however, because he has defined "technological man" as the one in control of science and technology; as standing above science and technology, not under it. Logically, then, Ferkiss is left with the old humanist dictum, "Man is the measure of all things," and in this case, Ferkiss is *the* man.

In his more recent book, *The Future of Technological Civilization,* the term "technological man" is less conspicuous, but Ferkiss's answer to the question—whence the source of values?—is a more complicated version of the same. He argues that nature itself provides the values according to which we should live. If we learn what nature "is" then we will know what we "ought" to do. He is at first convincing but a closer look reveals that he has simply shuffled the shells and relocated the pea. He emphasizes that humanity is at one with nature (holism), but says that nature apart from humanity promulgates no values. It is only through humans that values appear on the stage of evolutionary history. Nature is the source of value because humanity is. In effect, then, humanity still comes out the measure of all things.[35] And if "ought" is based on "is," then we are simply stuck with present bourgeois-industrial values, because the future "technological man" does not yet exist.

Nevertheless, Ferkiss is brave enough to offer a value system for us to try on for size, and it is a sensitive and insightful suggestion at that. He has recently labeled it "ecological humanism."[36] The first element in this new philosophy is what might be called the *new naturalism,* which asserts that humanity is in fact part of nature rather than something apart from it. This has implications for ecological decision-making. If we see ourselves as a part of the natural world and not as autonomous lords above it, and if we value the harmony between ourselves and nature, the justification for brash human triumphalism which upsets the balances of our ecosphere is undercut.

There will be a new priority established in which the care of the whole will become our primary concern.

This brings us immediately to the second and interrelated tenet of the new philosophy, a *new holism*. This is the realization of how interconnected everything is. Drawing from the school of Process Philosophy, Ferkiss discards the older mechanical picture of the universe as a bunch of "things" being manipulated by natural laws. To him, the universe as a whole is a single organic system and constantly in process. No part has any meaning outside its reference to the whole; no part can be defined or understood save in relation to the whole. This includes the human race. All people are linked with each other and with their social and physical environment in a fantastically complex moving equilibrium. To value anything properly, then, would mean to see it in light of the whole; concern for one person's destiny is simultaneously concern for the whole of humanity.

The third element of the new philosophy is the *new immanentism*. Something that is immanent is something that is within, in contrast to something transcendent which is out or beyond. Immanentism rejects the idea of a transcendent God, traditionally said to be "up there" or "out there." All life is part of a single system unto itself, and the ground of our meaning must be found within and not beyond the system.

We should note that when Victor Ferkiss argues that people are part of a larger whole, that whole being called "nature," he is not oblivious to the religious implications of this recognition. He says not only that nature provides the source of our value system but in addition that we should value nature for its own sake. The problem with the liberal and industrial mind-set is that they see nature as only of instrumental value, something to be used for purely human purposes. Even contemporary ecological rhetoric is a thinly veiled example of the instrumental evaluation of nature: we seek unpolluted air, natural foods, and conservation of the earth's resources not out of respect or love for nature but really to preserve the human race. But Ferkiss contends that nature should be valued for its own sake as something that exists for purposes other than ours.

People who are devoted to nature take pleasure in the simple fact of the existence of wilderness areas and living creatures that they, and perhaps even other human beings, may never see. This is akin to wishing well to people you will never meet. In this context, "respect and love are the only proper terms" to describe the appropriate attitude toward nature. We hardly need to apply our hermeneutic here because Ferkiss himself says that we are now going "beyond the level of science to that of religion."

> It is vitally important to human identity and the restora-
> tion of human society that human beings learn to re-
> spect, preserve, and interact with nature without hostility
> or greed, and this in turn means that nature must become
> once more in some sense an object of piety. He who
> seeks his life shall lose it, and he who abandons it shall
> find it is one of the most profound paradoxes of Chris-
> tian scripture. By the same token, only if we regard
> nature as valuable in itself can it come to be a source
> of value to humanity. A sense of oneness with nature
> and a realization that nature places limits on the pos-
> sibilities of human history—both individual and social—
> can only become the basis for social structures and
> policies if we stop thinking of nature as something to be
> coerced, as in magic, but rather as something to be
> revered as in religion. To do so is not to downgrade our
> own humanity but to enlarge it, to become more fully
> human.[37]

John Platt introduces a new philosophy of values into the discussion, one very much akin to that of Victor Ferkiss; but his analysis of who is at fault in the present crisis in values differs from that of both Bell and Ferkiss. Platt blames the value system of organized religion. Recall that Ferkiss blames the bourgeois-industrial values of liberal society and Bell blames *post*-industrial hedonistic values. But Platt says that though at present the belief systems of the major religions are based on many inspiring ideals, in practice they are also ridden with irrelevant, immoral, and dangerous concepts that damage our attempts to build a worldwide human society that can survive. What bothers Platt about the churches is "their male-dominated resistance to equality for women, [to] the right to di-vorce, [to] birth control, [to] the equality of minorities and 'heathen' outsiders, and their attitudes toward war, toward nature, toward property and land reform, and their food taboos, clothes taboos, and Sabbath taboos."[38]

In answer to the question of what values we must hold in order to survive, Platt lists four. First, we must have an ecological ethic that begins by recognizing our oneness with nature. To protect nature is to protect ouselves. On the personal side this means having no more than two children per couple, recycling our bottles, and leaving the land healthier biologically than we found it.

The second value is a belief in the human-potential concept, i. e., we need to provide for the development of every human being to her or his full potential if we are to create a humane society for the future. It emphasizes each person's need for love, and the need to redevelop openness and honesty and simplicity of life independent of consumer goods.

The third is existential responsibility. Platt rejects completely any notion of a divine hand influencing the course of human history; we are alone. We will be what we make ourselves. In classic humanist tradition Platt sees humanity as not only the measure but the maker of all things. He urges us to take our responsibility seriously.

The fourth leg of the table is belief in a "cybernetic working through." Basically, this means think ahead. We must proceed toward the future continually evaluating and re-evaluating, choosing and acting, with lookouts and feedback-monitoring as we work through current problems and continually adjust our human course in the light of new dangers or new possibilities. This cybernetic view of society he says is not subject to factionalism—it does not devolve into a contest between rich versus poor, liberal versus conservative, capitalist versus communist—it is rather "Human and Forward."[39]

But, we might ask, is "human" necessarily "forward"? This is the eschatological problem. On the basis of the human race as we have known it in the past and as we know it in the present, is there any ground for setting priorities founded on values other than the competitive selfishness of our bourgeois and consumptive society? Futurists such as Bell, Ferkiss, and Platt present us with the vision of a value system that differs from our own, and at times it is a grand and inviting vision at that. But because it is at variance with the present dominant system of values, on what basis can it be dubbed the genuinely human system? Can it be more than the mere projection of a few dreamers? We must examine the strengths and weaknesses of the strictly humanistic vision of the future; then the relevance of an eschatological vision of God will become more clear.

7
THE HUMANIST ALTERNATIVE

In the process of forecasting the future our futurists operate with a picture of what has come to be designated a "human" world. Alternative futuribles require us to make decisions; decisions depend on priorities; priorities presuppose values; and the implicit values of futurology seem to be oriented vaguely around the inherent goodness of people, and sometimes of nature. In the literature of futurology, the concept of humanization appears often.

In the present chapter I wish to draw attention to this emphasis on "the human" and analyze its role in futuristic thinking. I contend that humanism, either salient or silent, is philosophically unsupportable yet practically valuable. It fails to ground satisfactorily the values we need to embrace for our planetary future, yet the obvious concern of contemporary humanists for the welfare of all on our planet makes them appropriate allies for Christian futurists.

The assumption made by Ferkiss and Platt, along with Toffler, Reich, Theobald, and countless others, is that we want to make the future more "human." Though exactly what is meant by "human" is somewhat vague, some features are discernible. The truly human has a particular social, spiritual, legal, and moral character.

John Julian Ryan presents it this way:

> In short, a truly humane society would be one in which the primal rights of every man as a full human being would be respected as sacred, not the least of these being his right to lead a meaningful creative life as a worker serving others skillfully, personally, and honorably.[1]

Charles Reich describes the human society of the future as one that will take the

> form of community in which love, respect, and a mutual search for wisdom replace the competition and separation of the past, and a liberation of each individual in which he is enabled to grow toward the highest possibilities of the human spirit.[2]

Such a utopian vision of a future community of people characterized by love, respect, and personal liberty rather than selfishness and competition has a beauty that is rivaled only by apocalyptic visions. Futurists believe such a future is possible if in the present we gain the proper understanding, make the proper decisions, and thereby gain control of our future. It seems assured that if *humans* control the future it will be *humanized*.

From the above analysis, some questions emerge. First, what is the basis for asserting that this kind of a future is better than any other kind? I am not suggesting that a non-humanized future would be better; rather I am searching out the ground for the value judgment that a humanized future is better than some other kind. Given the first factor in our future consciousness, namely, dissatisfaction with the present, the humanized future we seek must logically differ from the "de-humanized" present. But is not the present state of affairs in some degree the result of human choice and control? Some people, if not all of us to some extent, live by priorities and values that differ from love, respect, and personal liberty. Many decisions and commitments are made because such things as money, power, prestige, exploitation, self-preservation, influence, and dedication to technological progress are held in great esteem and valued as good. On what basis can a futurist claim that values such as love, respect, and personal liberty take precedence over selfishness in futuristic decision-making? The scientific futurists themselves have defined their task as one of laying out alternative possible futures. The decision as to which future we will commit ourselves to is a political, ethical, and, yes, even a religious decision. It is my thesis, finally, that a vision of the transcendent kingdom of God—grounded in religious hope and trusting faith—in combination with secular projections for a "human" utopia, is necessary to project a solidly based yet vital image of a truly human future. This means that the noble visions projected by humanists are in need of further completion.

Humanists come in both pessimistic and optimistic varieties, as we have seen. Almost all accept the possibility that faced with the crises ahead we have the opportunity to destroy all of humanity, leaving the universe to roll on for eons without a conscious trace of our presence. In spite of this, most humanists are confident that we have the capacity or the potential to fulfill our highest ideals and rise to new and as yet unforeseen levels of moral and technical achievement. Their sermons, like the sermons of the religious preachers they so abhor, are always *musty*. We "must" do this, or we "must" do that, if we as a human race are to shoulder our responsibility and guide the course of events towards a humanized future.

The doctrinal statement of those seeking to represent "official humanism," *Humanist Manifesto II,* projects the goal of a future world community that transcends the divisiveness of national sovereignties, unites all sectors of the human family, renounces violence as a means for solving disputes and makes war obsolete, perceives humanity as part of the ecosystem and avoids unnecessary exploitation of natural resources and pollution, eliminates poverty in the world, reconciles competing political and economic systems, and fosters the self-actualization and fulfillment of the potential of each individual. That sounds great, but how do we get there from here? The *Humanist Manifesto II* answers: through understanding, decision, and control. It says we must "extend the uses of the scientific method" to gain an understanding of our situation, and that when "confronted by many possible futures, we must decide which to pursue"; it then enlists all people's "cooperative skill to implement this commitment in the decades ahead." Humanism clearly decrees that we will have to actualize this utopian vision *on our own;* we are the only ones who can make our dreams come true. The manifesto reiterates: "we can discover no divine purpose or providence for the human species. While there is much that we do not know, humans are responsible for what we are or will become. No deity will save us; we must save ourselves."[3]

This raises again the eschatological problem: if at the present time we are in a mess that we ourselves created, what basis is there for expecting that we will be able to save ourselves? And the frequent use of clichés, such as "we will make the future more *human,"* only confuses matters. If it is in fact the case that we alone are the determiners of our own destiny, then we must be responsible for what we are today. By our actions in the past we have already defined what is human. The theologian calls a spade a spade: people are sinners. The humanist shrinks in the face of this reality. The hope that we alone have yet to make ourselves *truly* human, that we will soon take the "step to man" or to "technological man" is without foundation and will soon be recognized as the mere utopian dream that it is. The Christian gospel in contrast, founded on trust in the transcendent future of God, pronounces forgiveness of sin and promises divine power to establish what we on our own are unable to do.

But before we get any further into theology, let us make a brief philosophical analysis of the humanistic vision of the future, which will reveal its inadequacy for achieving the desired end; that end being to provide a holistic vision of the future which will be of such deep ultimate concern that it could integrate the world's people around the priorities of survival and fulfillment for all.

The humanist faces a logical dilemma over values. By placing humans rather than God at the center of things, humanists must believe either that the human race will last forever or else that nothing has ultimate value. Despite John Platt's forecast that we might find a way to keep ourselves alive for "thousands or millions or billions of years," the discoveries of astronomy and the law of entropy predict the eventual uninhabitability of our planet and even the universe. It may take a long time, but things will come to an end; our universe is not eternal. If the humanists accept the fact that our race is not eternal, they must look forward to a time when all of our achievements will be exactly as if they had never been.

Of what value then is value, of what importance is importance, what meaning is there to all humanity's joys and sorrows once consciousness has vanished? If the humanist prescription for achieving survival and fulfillment consists in projecting a positive image of the future that issues out of our subjective imagination, how can that presumption grip people with the dimension of ultimacy? On what grounds does it become convincing that we should sacrifice today on behalf of the survival of our children or children's children in the next century? Why is not self-indulgence equally as legitimate? Sooner or later all will come to naught anyhow; why wait? The philosopher Charles Hartshorne says, "The thought of the world's end cannot encourage the will to life, but only the will to death— if there could really be such a thing. The only rational effect of the thought would be to paralyze our entire being."[4]

If we insist that the humanistic concerns we express are ultimate values, then we do so in the very face of evidence to the contrary. At best we affirm the ultimacy of ourselves. The only source or ground for value in the humanist system is the arbitrary will of the individual human being. That which has worth for us has been chosen by us. Our own subjective inclinations or preferences establish ultimacy. This amounts to ascribing infinity to ourselves even though we are finite; it is making something human into something divine. This Paul Tillich observes is *hubris* or human pride; it is idolatry.[5] Charles Hartshorne sums up the dilemma:

> Thus the alternative to religion in the true sense is megalomania in some form, the deifying of something human; or else it is the discouragement of man's vital impulses by the notion of an absolute so alien to man that he can derive no sympathetic satisfaction, no participating joy and fellowship from its existence, but must rather seek to annihilate himself as irrelevant to ultimate value.[6]

The net effect of humanistic values—floating on top without a transcendent grounding—is that they are too weak to integrate society or culture on their own. As we noted before, it is one's ultimate concern that centers and coordinates all the elements of one's personality. If the good of the whole is something less than ultimate, subject only to a cosmic oblivion more final, then any projection of a desirable world future becomes the groundless product of my own creative imagination. And if it is the product of my own imagination, then I am master of it and not servant. That ultimate concern which will finally claim the allegiance of a culture, and provide the society with a point of orientation around which it can organize its various elements, will do so only if it can claim the separate and autonomous concerns of each individual within. But with humanism all individuals can justify "doing their own thing" and forsaking any dedication and sacrifice for the good of the whole. Thus humanism fails to integrate the individual with humanity as a whole.

Humanism also fails to integrate people with nature as a whole. This synthesis is inhibited by humanism. Logically, the humanist can deeply love only humanity; but we know now that the full realization of humanistic ends must embrace all of nature. The belief in human autonomy is based on our superiority complex over everything else, both God and nature. "Of course the humanist can feel the beauty of nature and experience curiosity concerning it, but there is nothing in his theory to exalt these experiences to love, properly so called; that is, sympathetic identification with, living the life of, another sentient or rational being." To the extent that humanists approach this all-embracing attitude of love, which is "the only complete integration of thought and emotion," Hartshorne argues, "they will also approach theism."[7]

Persons of deep religious conviction affirm that it is God who created each of us. He also created other people, other animals, other things, all that is. The ground and center of our being is not located within each of us, but beyond us, in the loving will of the divine. It is this same loving will that is responsible for all of nature. To affirm theism is to affirm the priority of God over myself and to begin to appreciate and care for his creation as he does. It is to shift the center from humanity to something greater and more comprehensive.

The anthropocentricity of an ethical system based upon the humanistic program shows its impotence on the question of protecting the endangered species on our planet. Our descendants may never see the white seals of Canada or the alligators of Florida. But how can we convince the western sheepherders that the endangered eagles that cost them a portion of their profit should be legally defended against hunting rifles? If the only appeal is to some *human* interest, then when the chips are down preservation of the birds of prey and the bearers of exotics furs or hides will quickly take a lower rung on our ladder of priorities. To say that any diminution in nature diminishes each one of us is at best attractive sloganeering.

A serious valuing of nature requires religious grounding, and according to philosopher Frederick Ferré Christian faith is better equipped than humanism to cope with the problem of endangered species in nature. He writes, "The Christain consciousness can answer these questions less awkwardly, more directly, than the purely anthropocentric modern ethic will allow. The Christian can reply simply that golden eagles should be valued because God created them a species and still cares about them."[8]

Of course the humanists we meet and talk with daily may (or may not) be sensitive to the loss of the golden eagle or any other species. If they are, then we should applaud them. The point here, though, is that there is insufficient grounding for this concern if we rely only upon a humanistic philosophy. Preserving eagles as opposed to neglecting them could be simply one person's preference, very much like preferring hot dogs as opposed to hamburgers. There is no compelling reason to change my mind if my values are determined only by me and my preferences.

§

The point of departure for humanism is found in two closely related principles. First, humans are evidently alone in the universe, dependent for friendship upon their own kind. Second, just to recognize this aloneness will itself aid rather than hinder the good life here on earth. This may even sever our oneness with nature. Exemplifying this hegemony of humanity over nature, V. F. Calverton writes,

> Man will find a new strength and a higher form of courage in viewing it [nature] as neither friend nor foe, but simply as an outer force or substance that he can convert into malleable forms which can be hammered and chiseled and cemented and harnessed in ways advantageous to his exploitation.[9]

Calverton is brutal and clear; other humanists are less harsh. Dewey, for example, advocated a pious sense of our dependence upon the forces of nature and of nature as a whole inclusive of us. Such a holistic emphasis as that advocated by Ferkiss has only recently come into vogue within mainline humanism, even though *Humanist Manifesto I* observed that "man is a part of nature" in 1933. Systematically, however, when humanity becomes the measure of all things, there is no impartial judge left to determine what is selfish exploitation of nature and what is not.

Curiously though, the humanists accuse religion of setting humanity over against nature. Perhaps an extra comment is in order here about the dominion over, and the exploitation of, nature. It has become fashionable since the late 1960s to blame the Judeo-Christian tradition for the impending ecological disaster. Lynn White, in his oft-quoted and oft-reprinted essay "The Historical Roots of Our Ecological Crisis," refers us to the notorious passage of Genesis 1:26–28 where God commands man to have "dominion" over the earth. White argues that on this passage Christianity established a dualism between humans and nature and insisted that it was God's will that we exploit nature.[10] Paralleling White and referring to the same Biblical text, Ian McHarg says dramatically:

> the Biblical creation story . . . in its insistence upon dominion and subjugation of nature, encourages the most exploitative and destructive instincts in man rather than those that are deferential and creative. Indeed, if one seeks license for those who would increase radioactivity, create canals and harbors with atomic bombs, employ poisons without constraint, or give consent to the bulldozer mentality, there could be no better injunction than this text.[11]

But do White and McHarg give the Bible a fair hearing? The Hebrew verb *radah,* translated "have dominion," appears elsewhere in the Scriptures and always with reference to human relationships. It may indicate the rule of a master over a hired servant or a chief officer over laborers. The stress is always on humane treatment; a Hebrew master is charged that he not rule over his hired servant "with harshness." (Lev. 25:43, 46, 53)

Of particular interest are a number of occurrences of the verb that appear in contexts having to do with the dominion a king holds over his subjects. Perhaps it would be helpful to get a picture of how the Bible understands kingship. The verb *radah* appears in Psalm 72, along with these passages describing the Hebrew king:

> May he judge thy people with righteousness,
> and thy poor with justice! [vs. 2] . . .
> May he defend the cause of the poor of the people,
> give deliverance to the needy,
> and crush the oppressor! [vs. 4] . . .
> For he delivers the needy when he calls,
> the poor and him who has no helper.
> He has pity on the weak and the needy,
> and saves the lives of the needy.
> From oppression and violence he
> redeems their life.
> [vss. 12–14]

What is important to note is that the Israelite king is expected to care for those over whom he rules. In fact, whenever the king began to exploit his subjects for his own selfish interests—King David taking Bathsheba and killing her husband (2 Sam. 11), King Ahab's confiscation of Naboth's vineyard (1 Kings 21)—a prophet of God appeared to accuse the king of failing to exercise proper dominion (Ezek. 34:2–4). To exploit rather than to care is to misrule. If it is on the model of Hebrew kingship that the author of Genesis conceived of human dominion over the earth, it was a model of caring for the earth rather than of harsh exploitation.

In addition, the Bible's picture of the relationship between God, humanity, and the earth is basically holistic. Nature itself tells of God's presence in it (Pss. 19:1; 89:11). The popular hymn, "This Is My Father's World,"written near the turn of the present century, sees nature alive with the presence of the divine.

> This is my Father's world, And to my listening ears
> All nature sings, and round me rings
> The music of the spheres.
> This is my Father's world: I rest me in the thought
> Of rocks and trees, of skies and seas,
> His hand the wonders wrought.
>
> This is my Father's world: The birds their carols raise,
> The morning light, the lily white,

Declare their Maker's praise.
This is my Father's world: He shines in all that's fair;
    In the rustling grass I hear Him pass,
    He speaks to me everywhere.[12]

There is certainly no license here to fill the "skies and seas" with toxic and radioactive pollutants or to take a crass bulldozer attitude toward "rocks and trees" and "the rustling grass." If God "shines in all that's fair" then the only reverent response is to appreciate and respect the natural world of which we are a part.

In the story of creation, the man is pictured as dependent on both nature and God for his very being. The man is formed from the dust of the ground, i. e., "man is a part of nature." But being thus formed, God breathes into him the breath of life, "and man became a living being." (Gen. 2:7) People are not truly human except as they express their organic oneness with both God and the natural world. God, humans, and nature together make up the whole as the Bible sees it.

It is not the Bible, then, but only a view of the exclusive autonomy of humans that can justify the "bulldozer mentality." The era of greatest exploitation, proceeding from industrialization, stands in the wake of the Enlightenment rise of humanism and the severing of humanity from the whole of things. The Jews and the Christians are not the only ones who should be censured for sponsoring our ecological crisis.

The problem with the humanist position is that when autonomous humans are placed at the center of things, the vision of the whole becomes systematically superfluous. The *new holism* sought by Victor Ferkiss becomes unreachable. And the futurists—both secular and religious—seem to be in agreement that a vision of the whole is vitally necessary if we are to survive in the future. John Platt and countless others are seeking an ecological ethics, a system of ethics founded on the principle that people are part of the larger ecosphere and not autonomous lords over it. The Club of Rome has demonstrated how decisions in one sector of the world system reverberate throughout the world. The one future of the whole world is our concern, and if it is to be considered at the level of ultimate concern, we must recognize its transcendent ground.

This is where religious faith is so important. We defined faith in chapter 4 as trust in the God of the future. Faith is reliance upon a future power that transcends present weakness; it is the apprehension of an absolute divine will that orients us and directs our efforts. To quote Paul Tillich again, "Religion, in the largest and most basic sense of the word, is ultimate concern. And ultimate concern is manifest in all creative functions of the human spirit."[13] The important decisions and commitments necessary to guide us into a humanized future cannot be made unless they issue from our ultimate concern. It is our ultimate concern that provides our basic moral aim, our fundamental criterion for deciding which course of action to take. And we cannot view our ultimate concern as a relative value. The vision of a single humanized planetary society has an absoluteness built right into it; other values such as self-assertion, imperialistic power, and exploitation are absolutely excluded. What ground is there for excluding some values in favor of others? Such a ground must be absolute. Theologians have traditionally called this absolute "God."

IN SEARCH OF A GROUND FOR VALUES

Secular future consciousness is unconsciously looking for such a religious grounding for values. Sometimes it is not even unconscious. Herman Kahn himself has said that the problems that must be faced are more theological than technological and that the remainder of this century ought to be given to the question of the meaning and purpose of life. If, as the futurists say, we have a choice of several futures, and if the one we have will depend on decisions we make now, what criterion are we to use in deciding? Where will the criterion come from? What is the source of value—the *summum bonum*—and how is it grounded in reality? What are the goals and purposes of human life?

Scientific futurology is technically unable to provide the source of value on its own. In its pure form it attempts to make value-free judgments about the facts. Consequently, we must seek an extra-scientific source of value in order to know how to decide between ultimate survival or self-annihilation, between ravaging nature of its resources now or striving for ecological balance tomorrow, between gluttonous self-indulgence or sharing our food production with the poor and the hungry. These are some of the alternative choices for the future that social science can propose to our planning committees, but it is not equipped to decide which plans we ought to make. As we have seen, however, most futurists do not stop at presenting the alternatives but rather push on to recommend a particular course of action. The value system to which they appeal must come from somewhere; usually it is either their own personal opinion or that of humanistic philosophy, which amounts to about the same thing. In either case, what they present as the right thing to do issues only from the subjective projections of people; and if two people were to disagree as to what we ought to do, there is no transcendent ground of value to which we may appeal in order to arbitrate between them. We are thrown into the relativity of conflicting values at a time when absolute decisions about the one future of humankind need to be made. Realizing this, our enthusiasm and dedication to action is subverted from within and an eviscerating cultural malaise overtakes us.

Modern pluralistic culture is in a dilemma now because, on the one hand, it assumes the validity of the doctrine of the relativity of values while, on the other hand, we are faced with making decisions on behalf of one single planetary society. The doctrine of cultural relativism—a doctrine rigorously adhered to by most who claim to be humanists—states that all values and mores have their meaning only within the cultural setting in which they are found and, therefore, there is no single value or absolute notion of what is good that applies to all people. The authors of a typical college textbook on sociology, Horton and Hunt, argue that "a trait is neither good nor bad in itself. It is good or bad only with reference to the culture in which it is to function."[14] This view correctly recognizes that the meaning or value of something depends upon the context of meaning in which it is found. But beyond this, the doctrine of the cultural relativity of values is riddled with internal contradictions. It assumes that its own truth—namely, "all values are relative"—is universally valid, thereby escaping its own relativity. The belief in cultural relativity is thought to stand above the relativity of our own culture out of which it grew. But such a concern could grow and flower only in a self-consciously pluralistic culture such as we have. In our culture we value as good someone who can say, "I disagree with what you say but I will defend your right to say it." By believing in relativity the professional social scientists are embracing this value native to our own democratic heritage. What the social scientists often fail to accept is that relativity itself may be relative only to us.

This criticism is strictly theoretical and represents one form of a familiar logical puzzle. How often on a university campus does one hear a sophomore (*soph* = wise; *more* = moron) say, "Everything is relative," to which another responds, "Is that absolutely true?" But there is a practical and more telling criticism to be leveled against the doctrine of cultural relativity, namely, it is divisive at a time when we should be seeking unity. If cultural relativity itself becomes valued, the consequent decisions and actions would tend to draw lines and harden borders between cultural units. It is a slippery and subtle doctrine because in the very act of showing respect for integrity it undermines the move toward a planetary civilization.

Horton and Hunt even believe that, if they can determine whether or not a particular trait functions to *harmonize* or *integrate* the culture in which it is found, they can make a "non-ethnocentric test" of the goodness or badness of that cultural trait. They are saying implicitly, of course, that the principles of harmony and integration are absolutely good, non ethnocentrically derived, values. In a sense, this is an extension of the relativity doctrine because it asks each culture to so thoroughly integrate itself that it defines itself over against all other cultures. Its integrity is supposedly intact if it does not yield to any universal or trans-cultural ideals that overlap with others. But if we agree that harmony and integration are good regardless of what culture they are found in, would we be agreeing simply because they are good on the basis of what is good in our own culture or because it is absolutely true for all people? This philosophical dilemma is one from which social science has yet to extricate itself.

I for one agree that harmony and integration are good, but I wish these to be applied not just to individual cultures but to the whole of humanity. As we saw in the last chapter, the trends taking us toward a single planetary society cause us to transcend the

particular cultural traditions out of which we have come. The boundaries between cultures were never really walls; rather, they served
as filters that allowed communicative sharing while stamping what
was communicated with a certain character. And in the present age
we are witnessing the progressive disappearance of many boundaries between cultures. The operative knowledge shared in technology and politics is diminishing the influence of the many religions
and traditional belief systems. Our bodies of knowledge and self-
understanding are becoming as interdependent as are our economic
patterns.

All this could be considered very good if we were to value
movements toward world integration and harmony. So belief in
cultural relativism has become counterproductive; by absolutizing
pluralism it stands blocking the way of what could be a new world-
embracing conceptual synthesis and system of values.

Future consciousness already thinks world. Those who prescribe
certain directions for our decision-making urge us to think in terms
of a single planetary society. Consequently, belief in the absolute
relativity of values is not only self-contradictory but also a hindrance
to raising questions regarding the trans-cultural vision of an integrated planetary civilization.

Among the priorities we may set in the face of the alternative
futures lying before us, there are some that positively embrace a
single future for all of humanity. The context of meaning is no longer
that of a single culture; it belongs to the whole human race on earth.
The validity of what we decide to do cannot be determined only
on the basis of the harmony or integration it produces *within* one
culture, because its immediate or ripple effects are international and
even global in scope. If the choices we are compelled to make are
choices between utopia and oblivion, they have an absolute character. On certain basic or ultimate issues, then, there is little room left
for dispute between one person's opinion over against another's.
Perhaps Horton and Hunt are correct in implying that harmony and
integration among people are absolutely good; it is just that now
we need to apply it to the whole human race, not just to one culture.

But on what grounds? It appears that we need a value system
that is rooted in a source unconditioned by the relativities of culture,

rooted in the same comprehensive reality that gives being and life to people of all times and in all places. We require a transcendent ontological ground for the values that will animate the setting of our priorities. Of course, the basic values will express themselves initially in sets of priorities that are culturally conditioned, i. e., appropriate to the particular time and place where planning is done. But eventually all must flow towards the unity that is our one future. Hence, the being of the future itself could provide the ontological foundation for our values and ethical decision-making.

The recognition that all people are participating in a single universal historical drama is the insight necessary to take us beyond the relativity of values. The apocalyptic picture can provide us with this vision. Apocalypticism has a doctrine of universal history that finds its unity in the one single eschatological future of God. God is both the beginner and finisher of all things; consequently, he alone can provide the ontological foundation for our value system.

8
TOWARD A PROLEPTIC THEOLOGY OF THE FUTURE

Theology is basically thinking about God. St. Anselm defined it as faith seeking understanding. What we are attempting to do in this book is think through the relationship between future consciousness and belief in God. It is the significance of God for the future that we are trying to understand.

The basic elements of Christian theology are two: first, the witness of Scripture to the events in the career of Jesus Christ; second, the contemporary experience of asking about the purpose in human living and action. We have discovered that future-oriented thinking implicitly seeks an ontological ground for holding values and setting priorities. What I propose to do in this chapter is to extend the discussion of the relationship between ontology and values and then offer some theological suggestions.

The theological position I plan to develop will be skeletal and schematic only. It is aimed more at pointing a direction than providing all the answers. It emerges out of one central conviction, namely, the apocalyptic vision and historical resurrection of Jesus reported in the Bible suggest a way of meeting the values problem raised in contemporary future consciousness. The ontological foundation for values is closely tied to the ultimate future which derives from its proleptic anticipation in Jesus Christ.

VALUES, ONTOLOGY, AND THE FUTURE

By an "ontological foundation" I mean that ethical values must be rooted in the very structure of being itself; their source must be reality as a whole and not simply the subjective imaginations of people who superimpose them upon the facts. Victor Ferkiss realizes this and seeks to derive our ethical "ought" from what "is" in nature. But if being itself is historical and dynamic in character, then the "ought" is not derived from simply what "is" but rather from what "is to be" in the future. Following Socrates, the good is that which we now lack and for which we strive. The good is that which we do not yet possess conclusively, that which we must still strive to realize. There is a built-in duality between present and future, then, because value refers to what ought to be but is not. Insofar as our image of what is good stands in front of us as obligation and judge, then it is not yet fully actual. There is now a split between value and present being, between God's law and present reality.

This split between value and being has been long recognized in ethical thinking, especially in Christian ethics, and sometimes to the detriment of genuine ethical concern for the world. For example, when God is identified as the source of value but believed to be so transcendent that his home is in heaven and not on earth, human concern becomes otherworldly. When what we value belongs to another world rather than the one in which we are actually living, our priorities revolve around such matters as not smoking, not drinking, and keeping our legs crossed so that we can escape the present world and go to heaven. The world can then be left to go to pot with full ethical justification. But of course that is not the intent of our transcendent God.

The idea of the eschatological kingdom of God complements the idea that the good is what people strive for, but it also repudiates the otherworldly ethic that shirks responsibility for our world. That which we value is the future of *this* world, not another. God transcends our present world not because he lives in another place, like heaven, but because he is coming in the future. The advent of his kingdom marks the transformation of our present reality.

There must be transcendence; God and his law must stand over against our present reality to some degree for there to be a value to strive for. If God were totally immanent, totally absorbed into the present being of nature, he could not provoke dissatisfaction with the present and the desire for a new humanity. In some sense

God must stand beyond the present state of affairs in order to criticize it, in order to render judgment and promise resurrection.

In the past, transcendence was understood spatially, not temporally. The idea that God lived in heaven with his angels "up there" or "out there" was a way of expressing God's transcendence using the so-called mythological world view. According to the mythological world view heaven was thought to be upstairs, hell downstairs, and the plane of human history in between. The separation of heaven from earth in this scheme provided the "distance" needed to express divine transcendence. However, with the appearance of scientific astronomy and space travel, Christians for the most part have sought other imagery to express God's otherness over against the world. As suggested in chapter 5 on time, the revelation of God in the Bible departs from that mythological picture in many ways. So perhaps a temporal image of God's transcendence would be more true to Scripture and to our modern world view as well. I submit that we can understand God's transcendence of humanity just as we can understand the future's transcendence of the present.

That transcendence can best be understood as the future itself. Carl Braaten states it: "God's transcendence can be conceived today as the absolute power of the future. He comes to us not 'from above' but 'from ahead.' "[1] If God is understood as the source of all being, "the creator of heaven and earth," and if our ethical values implicitly direct us toward the transcendent future, then perhaps our understanding of God is leading us to an ontology of the future.

ONTOLOGY AND THE KINGDOM OF GOD

Ontology is the study of being. Perhaps we should not look to the past in order to discover the source of the being of our universe. That is what myth and science do. They look to the past with the idea that if we can locate the origin of something we can explain it. But neither myth nor science understands the origin of our universe as a creation out of nothing. The Bible does. In mythology the gods create by reordering some primordial stuff and making cosmos out of chaos; modern science presupposes the eternity of atomic matter and simply looks back over a history of matter in changing forms. What both myth and science have in common is the belief that the past determines the present, that the locus of power in being is a push and not a pull. This certainly seems to be the case with the second law of thermodynamics, the principle of entropy, in which it is postulated that the transformation of potential to kinetic energy is a one-way street and eventually the universe will run down like a wound up alarm clock. For science as well as myth the past contains all potency and the future is basically *futurum.*

But our hermeneutic of future consciousness reveals that at a deeper level we experience the gravity of time in the future rather than the past. Time really draws us toward the "will be" rather than pushes us from the "has been." Therefore, if Christian eschatology sees a decisively *adventus* dimension to the future, perhaps we need to view the creation of the world as a pull rather than a push. It is our experience that to be real is to have a future; to cease to exist is to drop into the nonbeing of the past. Can we understand God's act of creation as coming from the future rather than the past? I believe we can.

We can begin by observing that God's being is equivalent to his kingdom. Recall that by "kingdom" I do not mean geographical territory but reign, rule, or lordship. God is "almighty." God without his rule or his lordship is something less than God. To rule is to have power, and by the term "God" we are referring to the one all-determining reality. Jesus taught that the rule of God belongs to the future; the kingdom is coming.

The power of creation is at the end, not the beginning. God did not create the world once upon a time as a watchmaker creates a watch, winds it up, and then lets it run. Rather, creation is still going on. It is a process of being drawn toward a final future where everything will come into its full being as God's will determines it. The garden of Eden does not refer to a pristine paradise of long ago to which we eventually want to return; it is rather a dramatic vision of God's will for the future reconciliation of all people, and stands over us as judge and promise. Perhaps we can say that creation, redemption, and eschatology all focus on one thing: God, the future of all things.

It is the future of God that defines the being of things in the present. We have already seen how our vision of the future provides judgment upon the present and how the meaning of present events is determined by their place in the context of the whole of history, and that context cannot be ascertained until history is terminated. God's future is the power of creation drawing the reality of each thing towards its final definition, a definition to be determined only by its place in God's kingdom.

Hence, the concepts of divine power and world unity are futurized together. If the one God is the ultimate future of all people, then the consummate destiny of human activity is a final unity. Teilhard de Chardin is correct when he says that the world process is a movement toward the unity of all things at point omega.[2] Unless all things find essential unity in a single whole, God's power or rule is not final and the universe is still ruled by more than one god, by more than one contending power. The advent of the kingdom of God will terminate world history and draw it into a single whole— both temporal and spatial—which is the prerequisite to assigning the place and definition of all things within it. We have not yet become what we truly are.

But what about contingency and freedom? Are they not smothered by all this talk about future unity and wholeness? Quite the contrary, it is the power of God's future that is the condition for contingency and freedom. Recall that both myth and science assume that the power of being issues from the past and that the future as *futurum* can only actualize past potentialities. In effect, all that can be already is. Hopelessness would be the only logical consequence if genuine future consciousness limited itself to this view, because we would find ourselves imprisoned by what has been. The weight of the past would crush us, tradition would smother creativity, and guilt over past sins would prohibit the zest for renewal.

If we understand the power of being as coming from the future, however, we can see that we are set free from the burdens of the past for fullness in the present. The *has been* is constantly relegated to nonbeing by the power of the *not yet*. Each present moment enjoys release from the absolute determinism of the past when that past ceases to exist. The past of course has set us in our present physical and cultural context, but the power of God's future liberates human freedom for choice among a welter of new possibilities. The creation of freedom and contingency coincides with the age-old Christian contention that love is the ultimate motive of God's creative activity. The answer to humanity's most basic philosophical question—"why is there something and not nothing?"— is love. Christian theology affirms that God creates out of nothing; he is not constrained to do so by any prior conditions or dictates. God freely reaches out, "calls into existence the things that do not exist" (Rom. 4:17), seeking fellowship with the fruits of his creative power. But he grants to finite existence freedom, just as we in love must grant freedom to our beloved. To deny the beloved his or her freedom is to deny that person's personhood; it is to make him or her into a mere object to be exploited. Hence a love relationship is contingent upon the freedom of both the participants. God's future kingdom will be a fellowship, not a dictatorship.

Of course, genuine human freedom and the contingency of events opens up the possibility for evil. Evil we may define as the choice on the part of individuals to seek to absolutize their own being and alienate themselves from the projected unity of the whole, that is, to choose selfishness rather than love. We certainly do not need hard-nosed theology for this picture of evil; humanistic futurists such as Ferkiss and Platt have clearly shown how the selfishness of the economic and political institutions of today is the source of division and alienation that prevents the emergence of a single planetary civilization. Our present problems could be solved if humans were good by nature, seeking their satisfaction only from the common good, and not using everything for their own self-interest. Even though God's law is available to us in the form of a vision of what he wills for his future kingdom, the fact that we are free from the absolute determination of the past, combined with the fact that the future is not yet, means we can choose a path that deviates from that will. We are free to seek to thwart God's intention for a future unity of all things by seeking to maximize and absolutize the meaning of our own present. The result is a detour, a denial of God's being, and hence death. If God's future kingdom is the ground of being, whatever does not finally participate in it recedes into the nonbeing of the past, into death.

But judgment and death are met by the gospel promise of

resurrection. For God to overcome the alienation and destruction wrought by human evil and judged worthy of death, humanity must be transformed through resurrection. And if God's ruling lordship necessitates the final unity of all things, then all human individuals should be granted a share in that perfect society. The unity of all people does not refer simply to all those who happen to be living on that day when the curtain comes down on the stage of history. That would be something less than true unity and relegate all past preparations to meaninglessness. No, God's kingdom is consummation, fulfillment. It is *adventus,* but it still maintains continuity with the past and present in order for the creation to have wholeness rather than merely an end. It will require a resurrection of the dead to have all human individuals of all times participate in the perfect society. Resurrection then is not a post-death catapult into eternal individuality. Humans are social animals and even their individualities are not their own apart from relationship to others. Redemption must be for society if it is to be for individuals. The sign, the promise, the precedent, the pre-actualization, the proleptic anticipation of that final resurrection is available for our view in the resurrection of Jesus Christ.

Therefore, God's eschatological kingdom is not only a creation but a reconciliation and a redemption of all those individuals who chose defiance of his will. The eschatological problem, recall, was the question of how a human society in which the members are alienated from God and from each other could on its own power transform itself. The solution is that the transformation like creation itself is dependent upon God's power. God's rule is in the process of becoming actualized, and—if God is really God—we can have confidence that one day in the future his "law will be written on our hearts" and the "wolf will lie down with the lamb." This achievement, because it will come from God's power, we may call "grace."

GOD IS NOT YET GOD

What has been said thus far certainly has significant implications for our understanding of God. Long before the Russian cosmonaut traveled to outer space and acknowledged that he could not find God in the heavens, we had already accepted the fact that God could no longer be understood simply according to the mythological picture of the first century. We have had to translate the spatial imagery of myth, e. g., "heaven," into more abstract philosophical language, e. g., "transcendence." But must we give up every element of the first-century picture of reality in favor of the modern one? Can that first-century picture inform and enrich our own?

I am suggesting that the confirmation of the apocalyptic vision of the future through the resurrection of Jesus Christ may mean that we can hold on to the apocalyptic notion of time as historical. In fact, as I have already pointed out, the modern mind implicitly acknowledges this understanding. Here is a point of contact between the first and twentieth centuries that does not necessarily require demythicizing as does the spatial imagery.

With this in mind, perhaps we should delineate some of the implications this has for our understanding of God. I would like to set forth the following four theses for consideration.

Thesis 1: *God is absolute freedom.* To be free means to have one's future within oneself. To have only a past with no future is to be without freedom; it is to die. Freedom is best defined as the capacity to achieve a desired future state; it is the power to consciously realize one's goals as projected in one's image of the future.

The predominant notion of freedom that comes to us from eighteenth-century liberalism is that freedom is the absence of restraint. The concern then as now is to prevent any king or church or other power external to myself from telling me what to do. Freedom to the liberal Western mind means absence of control. But this is a naive view based on an outdated understanding of the individual as an isolated atomic unit with native integrity. Modern social science has demonstrated that the constitutive elements of our personalities are in large part due to external influences, e. g., the introjected values and neuroses of our parents and surrounding culture, etc. Individuals in society are interdependent for their very self-identities.

Freedom cannot mean absence of control. We are contingent beings. We not only act, we react. Whenever we react in response to the anticipated action of forces outside ourselves, we are in a sense controlled by them.[3]

Freedom can better be defined as having the ability to determine and actually fulfill the choices we make for the future. The range of choices, the alternative options, are in large part determined for us by the present situation in which we find ourselves. Choices are between concrete alternatives given us by the real world.

So also for God. God's future is for *this* world. Transformed, yes, but nevertheless it is for the present world of which we are a part. God's will does not operate in a vacuum. It has an object and a purpose, us.

What determines freedom, then, is not the contingent nature of one's point of departure. It is rather the power to actualize one's projected will for the future. This God has. And God has freedom absolutely because his will for the future will become absolute in the eschaton.

Thesis 2: *God creates from the future, not the past.* The more traditional or orthodox view is that God himself is eternal, and that at one point he created our world out of nothing, *creatio ex nihilo.* Creation took place at the beginning. It happened once and for all a long time ago. The being of the world at present is the repercussion of a great big push from the past.

But as I have suggested above, it makes more sense to view creation as a constant process of drawing reality towards the future and away from the past. It is a setting us free from the smothering determinism of an oppressive past and an opening up of the possibility for new ways of being in the future. Each moment is a dynamic process of the present slipping into the nonbeing, the *nihil,* of the past and the embracing of a new phase of reality that previously did not exist.

A further implication of this view is that the doctrine of redemption is collapsed into that of creation. The more traditional view is dualistic. It assumes that creation came first. It was followed by the fall into sin. Redemption then comes to return sin-infected creation to its original, pre-fallen state. It is a kind of return to lost paradise. This understanding is more consistent with the primitive mythical world view.

However, when we put both the source of creation and of transformation in the same place, the future, then the dualistic division becomes nonessential. God has one will for the future. Evil and sin have less reality than goodness and love because they are not ultimate; they will not endure into the final consummation. Evil is a present threat, to be sure, but at the advent of the eschaton it will pass into the dead past, into nonbeing. Division and plurality are being drawn into a final harmony and unity. Creation and healing are finally one and the same process. The universe will not be what God intended it to be until it is healed and fulfilled, i. e., until it is redeemed.

This calls for a new interpretation of the creation account in Genesis. The interpretation I suggest here I hope does justice to both the ancient text and contemporary consciousness. The important element in Scripture that we should focus on is the claim that God creates and redeems through his Word.

In Genesis 1:1—2:4a the cosmos comes into being in response to God's Word. He says, "Let there be light" and light comes into existence. So also for the rest of the furniture of our terrestrial living room: dry land, plants, fish, animals, birds, and humans. The result is the garden of Eden in the subsequent chapters, a garden that has been nicknamed "Paradise." The creation is reported completed just as God had intended it. It is perfect.

But we admit that nobody today lives in exactly that garden. And if we assume the validity of evolutionary theory, then nobody ever lived in the garden in the past either. If the garden is real yet neither past nor present, then perhaps it is future.

If we think of the creative power of God as dynamic and not static, then God is in the continuing process of creating. He did not create everything once and for all and then quit. We are still living in the world of Genesis 1 where God is speaking. Genesis is a book written to us in the present and directing our attention toward the future. The garden of Eden is yet to come in its fullness.

The idea of God's Word in process also applies to the concept of redemption. The first chapter of John in the New Testament recalls the original creation account.

> In the beginning was the Word, and the Word was with God, and the Word was God. He was in the beginning with God; all things were made through him, and without him was not anything made that was made. . . . And the

> Word became flesh and dwelt among us, full of grace
> and truth; we have beheld his glory, glory as of the only
> Son from the Father. [John 1:1–3, 14]

Note that here Jesus Christ the redeemer is identified with the selfsame Word of God that brings all of reality into existence. There is continuity between God's original intention in creating the cosmos, the incarnation of his will in his Son, and the consummate fulfillment of all things in the eschaton. Perhaps a revised picture of God's Word is necessary to bring these things together.

The Greek term for "word" in the Gospel of John is *logos*. *Logos* implies more than simply "word." It is the rational principle ordering and organizing all reality. It is the mind of God working within the things of the universe guiding it toward its divinely appointed destiny. Thus, the Word of God as *logos* is not spoken in a once-for-all fashion as is a human word. When we speak there is a momentary sound which may echo in our minds for a while; and sometimes the words of a great thinker will influence cultural developments for a considerable period. Nevertheless, we think of our words as transient. Once spoken they disappear. They may be repeated or forgotten, but they do not themselves endure.

In contrast, God's Word is eternal. Thus, he did not just speak once in the past to set things up in the world and then return to silence. God is still speaking. Perhaps we can imagine God as having opened his mouth to emit the sound, and that sound is still coming forth centuries and millennia later. He will not close his mouth and finish his speaking until everything is fully created, until all things find their consummate fulfillment in his eternal kingdom. Creation, redemption, and consummation are all the work of the one Word of God. He is still calling us into being.

The power of being is most deeply experienced as the draw of the present out of the past and into the future. It also makes solid theological sense to say God creates from the future, not the past.

Thesis 3: *God is not yet God*. In most religions what designates divinity is power. The gods of primitive polytheism were defined initially by their function in nature: the sky-god had power over the rain, the earth mother goddess had power over the fertility of the soil, etc. With the emergence of monotheism all such powers were consolidated under a single deity. One god became tagged as the author of creation and the sole source of its continuation and preservation. In the classical Christian doctrine God is omnipotent, i. e., has total power.

Following this line of thought, then, "God" must be equivalent to the "kingdom of God." To be the God of Christian doctrine, he must reign completely. His will must be totally realized throughout his domain, and his domain is the whole of reality. The eschatological vision of the New Testament says that this kingdom is coming. It is the not yet which draws us out of the present and towards our consummate fulfillment. God is not yet God in the fullness of his kingdom.

God's omnipotence is the absolute "will be" that transforms our contingent "is-ness" into a "was-ness" and frees us for a "yet to be." The power of God's future reality is effective in the present, but it is not to be equated with the present. God transcends the present as the future does. Nevertheless, it is this world which is the domain of God's rule, and that rule has yet to be fully realized. The "is" of all things is present tense. If reality takes its bearing from what will be, then "to be" now is to be on the way but not yet fully there.

In this regard Wolfhart Pannenberg argues, "Thus, it is necessary to say that, in a restricted but important sense, God does not yet exist. Since his rule and his being are inseparable, God's being is still in the process of coming to be."[4] What Pannenberg intends by this statement is to assert that God has yet to materialize in his fullest identity and magnitude. In this sense, I concur with Pannenberg.

The nature of God's existence needs further clarification. If we press the notion of existence, perhaps it would be better to say that God now exists but he is not yet fully actual. I am thinking here of the notion of existence as it appears in Existentialist philosophy. We are told by the Existentialist philosophers that what makes us *persons* rather than mere *things* is that persons can project themselves imaginatively into the future. Things—in contrast to persons—are simply here or there; things do not project themselves into worlds as yet unknown. If we were simply to accept our lot in life as that of being at one with our surrounding environment, to see ourselves only as part of the furniture of the world, then we would deny our true freedom and our true humanity. To be human is to *exist*. The word "exist" comes from two Greek words which mean "stand out." Human beings are never completely at one with their present station in being; they "stand out" from their time and place by projecting themselves toward something that does not yet have being, namely, the future.

At present God exists as a project, as the thrust of the present beyond itself to something new. To exist seems to imply a duality within, a conflict between the person I am and the person I wish to be. This is the dynamic element in personality. In this sense God's personality is now dynamically at work in human history; he exists —he stands out—he projects. However, God is not yet an actual reality because he will not attain his full quiddity until his will becomes fully absolute in the eschatological kingdom. But then, this applies to all of us as well. All of reality is on the way to becoming its true self, God included.

This thesis is not in any way to give comfort to the death-of-God theologians or to spawn an interim atheism. The power of God is effective in the present; it is just not yet absolute.

By "kingdom of God" I do not refer to God alone, to God in his *a se* individuality. For God, like us, to be himself he must be in relationship. That is his will. His absolute power then is not a power that rules over against the subjects in his kingdom but rather in concert with them. It is a community of harmony and cooperation, not alienation and oppression.

With power goes authority. "Authority" is commonly thought to refer to the imposition of an alien will upon us. But, in fact, if the will of the so-called "authorities" must be imposed against our wills, it is a sign of diminished authority. The government that has to resort to domestic espionage and police power in order to enforce its will is one that has lost its authority with the people. True authority is received and accepted. The government that has genuine authority is the one that goes almost unnoticed, because its people so embrace its policies as expressions of the deep values they personally hold. It is only when the rulers' desires conflict with the values of their constitutents that they resort to force to impose their will. The sense of alienation between ruler and ruled is by definition absent from the kingdom of God. Recall Jeremiah's projection of a new community in which God's law will be written on our hearts. Revelation says there will be no need for a temple, because if God is everywhere there is no particular place we can go to enhance our relationship to him. God's being and our being will be interdependent and shared. God's power will be absolute, but it will be indistinguishable from our own. Both God and people will become fully at one with themselves together.

Thesis 4: *Jesus Christ is truly God.* The as yet future kingdom of God has already appeared proleptically in the person of Jesus. The fullness of God's reign has been actualized *intensively* in this one person. It now awaits its actualization *extensively* in all human beings and nature. Jesus Christ is the incarnate *logos,* the will of God at work under the conditions of human personality within the structures of the present passing eon. Jesus Christ is at one with the ultimate future; he is at one with the God who is yet to be.

It is this focus upon Christ that gives our proposed theology its proleptic character. As mentioned, by "prolepsis" I mean the antici-pation of future reality in a concrete pre-actualization of it. Jesus Christ proleptically reveals the destiny of the whole world because he embodies it in his own personal destiny.

Prolepsis is a temporalization of the traditional doctrine of the incarnation. To incarnate means to take on flesh, and the imagery in the first centuries of the Christian era was that of a disembodied spirit taking on a body. Note that this is basically spatial imagery. It presupposes the separation between body and soul, matter and spirit, earth and heaven. The Nicene Creed says the Son of God "came down from heaven and was incarnate by the Holy Ghost of the Virgin Mary."

What happens when we temporalize the incarnation and locate God's creative power at the consummation? We get prolepsis. Jesus Christ is the future made present. He is the first fruits, a foretaste of the great banquet yet to be enjoyed by us in the consummate kingdom of God.

This understanding of Jesus is derived by examining his Easter resurrection in light of the interpretive context in which it was first understood, namely, Jewish apocalypticism. By raising Jesus from the dead God was confirming as valid the widespread hope for the future kingdom of God. Many were expecting the course of world history to erupt into uncontrolled violence and catastrophes, with those loyal to God suffering unjustly at the hands of the enemies of God. Jesus experienced this in his own person as the mob and the government brought him to a cruel and unjust death on the cross. Many were also expecting a resurrection from the dead and a vindication of righteousness. Jesus experienced this too in his own person in a way that loosely fit the expectation. The New Testament message, then, proclaims that as Jesus rose so also will all of us who are tied to his destiny rise in the future. It becomes a message of joy and hope even when great calamities threaten to engulf us as they apparently do now.

Consequently, our vision of God's ultimate future should be informed by our knowledge of who Jesus was. The life and destiny of Jesus are a hermeneutical tool for interpreting our present relationship to the future. To affirm that Jesus Christ is at one with the creative source of all of reality means that he points the way toward the ontological ground for ultimate value.

9
CONCLUDING
NONSCIENTIFIC PRESCRIPT

If we want an ontological ground for our value system, that ground must be the future being of the kingdom of God. The point of contact between *adventus* and *futurum,* between hope and planning, is that our vision of God's ultimate future provides a foundational point for establishing what it is we value and what goals we ought to set. Scientific futurology may be able to forecast alternative possibilities, but, as Jürgen Moltmann reiterates, "Without specific goals towards which hope is directed, there can be no decision about the possibilities of planning."[1] Once we have a vision of what God intends for the ultimate destiny of humans, that vision can help us to set the priorities for the decision-making we must do in planning our immediate future.

SEDATIVE OR STIMULUS?

Hope for God's future is not a sedative but a stimulus to action. Prelates and theologians both Catholic and Protestant agree. Pope Paul VI, in an apostolic letter to Cardinal Maurice Roy in 1971, wrote: "the expectation of a new earth must not weaken but rather stimulate our concern for cultivating this one." And a renegade Catholic who is a thorn in the side of papal infallibility, Hans Küng, recently wrote: "It is by hope itself that the present world and society are to be not only interpreted but changed. Jesus did not want to provide information about the end of time, but to issue a call for the present in view of the approaching end."[2] And the pioneer Catholic theologian of hope and liberation, Johannes B.

Metz, contends that "hope itself liberates the element of active shaping the world" and that, because there is one God, we Christians should take responsibility for "the one promised future" of our world.[3]

Protestant thinker Langdon Gilkey argues that for both Protestants and Catholics ethical and political action originate with the eschatological vision. He writes: "Faith, hope, and love define man by specifying his *possibility* for the future under grace, a possibility that can only be realized or incarnated in actions in his world directed at a better future. Christian symbolism calls man into the future and into action in the world if he would become himself at all."[4] And Wolfhart Pannenberg sums it up: "the striving for God as the ultimate good beyond the world is turned into concern for the world."[5]

This vision of eschatology is not pie-in-the-sky-take-me-to-heaven-when-I-die escapism. Rather, once our hope embraces the vision of God's love at work in the creation and redemption of the world, our own love is triggered into action aimed at transforming the present in behalf of our image of the new.

Christians' love moves beyond the narrow horizon of their own happiness. They realize that the fulfillment of their own individual lives cannot be gained through exploitive self-interest but rather through the larger love that is God's affirmation of the world.

One cannot love God without also loving his creation; to attempt to do so is to misunderstand the nature of God. The key to understanding the inextricable connection between love for God and love for other people is the identity of God's being with the coming of his kingdom. God is not an entity living in some heavenly realm of his own, strictly transcending our world. Nevertheless, Christian ethics has often been mistaken about this—has often thought of the spatial language that contrasts our "vertical" love for heaven and our "horizontal" love for each other, as if they were two distinct and separate acts. But if God is at one with his rule and if his lordship consists in the realization of his will that we love one another, then the two loves become interdependent. Insofar as we dedicate ourselves to this double-directed love, the future becomes present and our actions themselves proleptically anticipate the final future.

Quite often Christian affirmations of the resurrection and the kingdom of heaven are met with hostile opposition in today's discussions. Otherworld-oriented religious piety has been sharply criticized by humanistic revolutionaries because it seems to sacrifice the present on behalf of an unattainable future. The 1973 *Humanist Manifesto II* contends that "promises of immortal salvation or fear of eternal damnation are both illusory and harmful. They distract humans from present concerns, from self-actualization, and from rectifying social injustices."

Marxism makes the same criticism. An otherworldly belief in heaven must be abolished, argued Karl Marx, because, although religion is evidence of people's dissatisfaction with the present, it makes the oppressed person a passive accepter rather than an active transformer of the *status quo*. In 1844 Marx wrote, "Religion is the sigh of the oppressed creature, the heart of a heartless world, just as it is the spirit of a spiritless situation. It is the *opium* of the people. The abolition of religion as the *illusory* happiness of the people is required for their real happiness."[6] Marx believed that religion would endure in human society only so long as there was a class structure with its accompanying oppression. Once the revolution came, once the ownership of the means of production was in the hands of the workers, then religion would simply wither away like dying leaves in October. If people could gain economic and material happiness in the present, they would no longer need the promise of spiritual happiness in the future.

But Marx's predictions about religion have not proven true. More than half a century after the Bolshevik revolution, and despite the strenuous efforts of the League of Militant Atheists, religion still lives in Russia. In the spring of 1977, Easter eve and Easter day liturgical celebrations were reported filled to capacity in the Soviet Union. This, despite a Kremlin-directed campaign to tempt Soviet citizens to stay away by allowing theaters to hold special showings of popular foreign films in competition with the services. Furthermore, Marx would be puzzled by what we call the "New Left" today. Not only are priests, nuns, ministers, and divinity students taking many of the leadership roles in movements for social transformation, e. g., civil rights, war protest, anti-poverty programs, ecological renewal, etc., but they are not ashamed to use exorcisms, sing hymns, and hold prayer vigils. Religion has not necessarily served to make these people passive.[7]

The religion of the American blacks is occasionally singled out as an example of an opiate or pie-in-the-sky religion. The black experience in the land of the free and the home of the brave is a history of chains, slaveships, being treated like property, servitude, long days in the hot sun, whippings, degradation, and resistance. So the slave looked forward to heaven as a place where the oppressed could "lay down dat heavy load," where "in dat great gettin' up morning" their present burdens would find relief. Black slaves sang:

> No more hard trial in de kingdom;
>   no more tribulation, no more parting,
>   no more quarreling, back biting in de kingdom,
> No more sunshine fer to burn you,
>   no more rain fer to wet you,
>   every day will be Sunday in heaven.[8]

Certainly there were many slaves and other Christian believers who literally waited on God, expecting him to bring salvation in response to their faithful passivity. But American blacks also sang "we shall overcome." James Cone argues that the pie-in-the-sky hope of Christian people does not necessarily function as an opiate. Rather, the religious vision of God's future heaven in radical contrast to the present state of oppression inspires hope, and hope provokes criticism and action.

> The partly revealed future of God, as disclosed in the cross and resurrection of Christ, made black people resist the condition of enslavement. Indeed, if the Kingdom was truly present in their midst, and if it was really ultimate, then they *had* to disobey all values that hindered their obedience to the coming Kingdom. Heaven then did not mean passivity but revolution against the present order. Against overwhelming odds, black people fought the structures of slavery and affirmed their membership in a "city whose builder and maker was God."[9]

Hope for an otherworldly future need not be a sedative but may be a stimulant to action.

The Christian church is to a large extent responsible for the revolutionary consciousness that is emerging around the world. Indirectly, through centuries of ministry and missionary activity, the church itself has provoked liberation consciousness by preaching a message that sets things in motion by stirring the imagination, arousing new expectations, and stimulating a crusading zeal to translate hopes, whose realization some would postpone for heaven above, into the social structures of this world now.

Carl Braaten says, "Christianity is a conspiracy for freedom"; but Christendom itself may not be aware of it.[10] The common reaction in the West is to attribute the spreading of revolutionary consciousness to communism, whereas in fact the communist understanding is a secularized version of the Jewish-Christian vision.[11] The church's antagonism toward the atheism and violence of communism makes it difficult for the church to see it as a bastard son, yet still a son. In addition, the church has prostituted itself by betraying the promises of the gospel for the sake of securing alliances with classes tenured with privilege, power, and position. While the gospel that Christians have preached points the way of hope for the future, the very institutions they built impeded its coming. Here lies the major reason for the anti-Christian character of modern revolutionary movements. But now we must urge Christian churches to repent of the inglorious role they have played in suppressing the spirit of social transformation. When the dynamics of the Christian gospel are released into the world, they set in motion waves of revolutionary expectations that threaten the structures of injustice and inequality. What a travesty if the Christian vision of justice in the future kingdom of God does not inspire visions of justice for this present world!

The result of this religious vision, then, is not merely to provide pie-in-the-sky-by-and-by acquiescence, but rather through criticism of the present to provoke enthusiasm for this-worldly transformation. Faith in the God of the future proclaims that the brotherhood of Consciousness III—to be brought about by abolishing economic exploitation—is possible, that efforts to reestablish an ecological balance are not in vain, that God calls us to just these tasks and assures us of their fulfillment. Thus the Christian vision of heaven has functioned not only as an opiate, inoculating the faithful against the pains that might stimulate action, but also as a vision of what will come to pass that brings criticism upon the present and fires enthusiasm for its transformation.

TOMORROW'S REALITY AND TODAY'S ACTION

The doctrine of the kingdom of God is not a detailed program for social and economic change. However, our understanding of the coming kingdom does inform and shape the planning required for particular situations. What then should the Christian church do to relate its vision of God's ultimate advent to our planning for the near future?

There are six basic things the Christian church can do that will make a significant contribution to our planning for the new world of tomorrow. (1) First and most important, it can *prophesy* visions of God's coming kingdom. In addition, the church should (2) *promote* a sense of global *Gemeinschaft* (community); (3) *provide* for our posterity; (4) *produce* programs; (5) *propose* alliances between Christians and non-Christians who share visions of a truly human future, and (6) *proclaim* pardon and comfort in the face of our failures to achieve by ourselves all that those visions require of us.

First, the church must *prophesy visions.* This might otherwise be called consciousness raising. Through word and deed the church can point humanity toward God's final future. That future will provide an ultimate ground for our value orientation and inspire the hope and enthusiasm we need to formulate the plans and take the action that will incarnate that reality in the continuing present. Where there is no vision of the future we must seek to provoke one; where there is already a vision, we must seek to deepen its concern and widen its scope to include all people. As we make more concrete the image of a society with God's law of love written on our hearts, our vision begins to stress priorities such as unity, peace, justice, the sense of brotherhood. Its scope is planetary, embracing the peoples and cultures of all places (and even all times). It values individual freedom and spontaneity, but not when freedom is used for competitive exploitation. It enjoins us to humanize technology, to put machines into the service of feeding, clothing, housing, and healing people who need such care. It also enjoins us to naturize or ecologize technology, to provoke respectful awareness of the machine's dependence upon the materials and principles of nature from which it came. We must put forth an image of spaceship earth as an organic unity, with God as the heart that animates and gives vitality to all.

Such a vision must have three additional characteristics. It must be positive, prophetic, and judgmental.

The visions of the future projected by the church should be basically positive, not negative. This is the case for two reasons. First, it is simply true that the ultimate future will be good. This is God's promise. Nothing else could be the content of Christian faith and hope.

The second reason is practical. Recalling what we said earlier about hope, positive images of the future have a greater potency for exciting the human will than do negative images. Fred L. Polak, sociologist at the University of Utrecht's Institute for Futurology, says that positive images of the future are the primary causal factor —though not the only factor—in cultural change.[12] Positive images of the future pull a civilization forward and unite the culture in a single task. Whether it is an eschatological heaven or a humanistic utopia, a positive image of the future excites the imagination and energizes the public will. It gives hope that present problems will be solved and inspires confidence in what is to come. The image of the future of a given civilization embodies the value structure that unites the culture and the moral goals toward which it strives. Harvard sociologist Daniel Bell contends that "In the end, it is moral ideas —the conception of what is desirable—that shapes history through human aspiration."[13]

Except in the case of a dire emergency, it is almost always easier to mobilize society around a positive rather than a negative image. The practical problem with the limits-to-growth scenario of exponential growth resulting in an inevitable catastrophe within the next century is that it projects only a negative image. It has a tendency to dampen morale; and it may even contribute to becoming a self-fulfilling prophecy if some are provoked to grab what they can now before it is too late to enjoy it.

Herman Kahn and the Hudson Institute are sharply critical of this negativism. It is just this negativism, they argue, that "creates low morale, destroys assurance, undermines the legitimacy of governments everywhere, erodes personal and group commitment to constructive activities and encourages obstructiveness to reasonable policies and hopes."[14]

Nevertheless, with regard to the work of the Club of Rome and others, we must still raise the question of truth based upon what we observe in present trends. The practical question ought not take priority over the question of truth. Herman Kahn agrees and contends that his own optimism for the future is based upon the facts; he says the limits-to-growth advocates also seek truth but they misinterpret the facts.

It is my own judgment that even if the limits-to-growth position is unduly pessimistic, it still raises to our consciousness the real challenges we must face. Industrial growth does destroy the environment; too many people for too little food does result in starvation; unnecessary competition between rich and poor does lead to violence. The very reason for projecting a positive image of the final future is to incite commitment and courage to meet these challenges. The vision of the final future gives us the ammunition to do battle with the challenges of the near future. The Christian can afford to confront the truth realistically without losing confidence.

One Christian theologian, Kenneth Cauthen, agrees that the single most powerful influence for generating cultural change is society's image of the future. Only a society that believes strongly in the future has a future. The vision that *should* provide the criteria for our priorities in decision-making and inspire our action, Cauthen says, is that of a "world community (1) consisting of a population within the biological carrying capacity of the planet (2) organized politically and economically in ways that provide to all human beings equal access to the means of material fulfillment and (3) organized technologically in ways that (4) neither exhaust essential natural resources of earth nor (5) upset the delicate balances of nature which make the environment capable of supporting life."[15]

Because great ideas do influence the course of historical events, then the very projection of such a vision by the Christian faithful will constitute a practical step toward bringing it to pass. Through such witness to God's future the power of that future itself will be at work in the present.

In addition to being positive, such visions need to be prophetic. To be convincing, they need to be ontologically grounded, that is, they must come from the mouth of God himself. We cannot, of course, simply choose to become a prophet and deliver oracles directly from God as Amos and Jeremiah did. This kind of (supernatural) prophecy is at the strict disposal of the Holy Spirit.

God has spoken through Scripture, however, and contemporary prophecy can pronounce the Word from God through a disciplined exposition of the Biblical message. The portent of God's future judgment is foreshadowed in the Deuteronomic recounting of Israel's kings and the challenges of the great Old Testament prophets. The apocalyptic vision of a new creation and a single reality-wide sanctified community of living things has been confirmed by the resurrection of Jesus Christ on Easter. Contemporary prophecy can take as its point of departure the unveiling of the future stages of human history found in Scripture.

That the vision comes from God is important. Recall we said earlier that being grasped by a sense of ultimate worth or transcendent value is the experience of the sacred; it is what constitutes religion. It is the religious dimension that provides ontological grounding for what we value. And unless such valuing is rooted in something that transcends our own subjective desires and arbitrary wills, it cannot grasp us as more ultimate than ourselves. Without transcendent ultimacy we will be unable to sacrifice for others and hence be morally impotent to meet the challenges posed by the future.

Christians need to project visions of a future that is both human and divine. It is God's future. It is our future. It is the future of our ancestors and our descendants, of our friends and our enemies, of those we know intimately and of those we have yet to meet. Because it is God's future it is ultimate. Because it is our future we are responsible for it.

A positive and prophetic vision of God's ultimate future lures us on to embrace it, but it also presents a vantage point from which to critically view the present. Such a vision is double-edged; it is both lure and judge. Jesus said he came to give life and to give it more abundantly. He also said he came not to give peace—an illusory peace—but a sword. This sword cuts through our illusions of peace; the lure of God's ultimate peace brings judgment upon the false dreams of the present.

Because the coming kingdom promises both personal and world fulfillment, it draws us to it. Awareness of it creates dreamers and doers dedicated to realizing its promises. Hope in God's future is a source of creative and inventive imagination in the service of love; it releases anticipatory thoughts and the drive to make life in the present more just, freer, and more humane. But at the same time it stands as a judge and critic of the present state of affairs. Even though Christianity has been intimately involved with the rise of industrial civilization, it still needs to step back and see how the value system of liberal bourgeois society is fundamentally selfish and destructive of human unity. The church seemed to be able to justify selfishness in the recent past because liberal industrialism presumed that growth was infinite, that competitive ambition increased the world's total wealth, thereby accruing to everyone's benefit. But now that the finite limits to growth are pressing in upon our awareness, we must see that selfish competition necessarily means that the spoils go only to the victor and that the poor and the downtrodden become poorer and more trodden under. Christian future consciousness must use its future vision to bring judgment upon the present values of the civilization of which it seems so inextricably a part.

The supplanting of bourgeois competitive selfishness with the mood of sacrificial sharing has been continually celebrated in the Christian eucharist. Jesus spoke of himself as the bread of life, as manna from heaven, given by God to feed our spiritual hunger. Jesus gave of himself, totally. In remembrance of him, liturgical Christians assert that they eat his body and drink his blood in the bread and wine of the Lord's Supper. All those dining, then, share the very being of Christ and become in a sense one body with him. This unity gained through the sacramental sharing of food could be a potent symbol for helping us to understand our responsibilities today, one of which in particular is the sharing of food.[16]

Recall that many of Jesus' parables tell of the Messianic Banquet in the future kingdom of God, and that one way of understanding the eucharist is to see it as tomorrow's bread given us today. The image of the great dinner suggests abundance, joy, fullness of life, and unity with one another brought by the atmosphere of merriment. The key that opens the entrance to the banquet hall is self-giving, whether it be that of Jesus Christ or us one to another.

One genre of pulpit illustrations which seems to be a favorite for many Christian preachers is the dream judgment scene. It usually begins with the story of a man who dreamed he had died and found himself standing before the pearly gates of heaven. The variations on the theme are legion; most are somewhat corny; but they do function to make the future judgment of heaven apply to the present situation. One example may be pertinent here.

In this case our nameless protagonist dreamed he had died and that his soul had successfully passed the judgment so that he was invited to enter heaven. He rejoiced at accepting this invitation, but his curiosity about the fate of the damned prompted a strange request. He asked St. Peter if he might be allowed one brief visit to hell before his final entrance into heaven forever. Although perplexed at this unusual request, St. Peter arranged with the celestial counterpart of Cook's Tours to have our hero guided through the netherworld.

As he approached the gates of hell, he could already hear the weeping, wailing, and gnashing of teeth. The moaning grew more intense the closer he got. Upon entering hell itself he discovered that it consisted of a gigantic dining room. The table was set for millions. It was graced with elaborate cut-glass candelabra, bone china with crocheted napkins, the world's finest wines served in jeweled goblets, hors d'oeuvre delicacies from every clime, a variety of entrées to satisfy the taste of every palate, a luscious line of desserts which had no end. Truly a sumptuous repast to be had.

However, there was a catch. Each diner was required to use only the six-foot-long chopsticks supplied by the host. The chaos was overwhelming. People simply could not feed themselves. The diners fought vainly with their two- or three-foot arms to guide the six-foot utensils to their mouths. The frustration at seeing such delectable food yet being unable to eat it caused universal anguish. This was hell.

Our hero had seen enough and requested that he be taken

directly to heaven where he belonged. When the gates swung open and he could see heaven for the first time he was dumbfounded. The scene was the same as that of hell. There was the same gigantic and luxuriously decorated table, the same beautiful hors d'oeuvres, entrées, and desserts. There was the same requirement that the diners use only six-foot-long chopsticks.

But there was a difference. Here there was no frustration, no weeping or wailing, no starvation. Here he found only joy, happiness, laughter, song, and fulfillment. The difference was that the diners in heaven were feeding each other.

§

Although prophesying visions of God's ultimate future is the primary contribution of the church, it should, second, make every effort to *promote a sense of global Gemeinschaft.* The term *Gemeinschaft* has been adopted by sociologists to refer to a group of individuals whose relationship with one another is characterized by a strong sense of common identity and closeness or intimacy. The family would be an example of a *Gemeinschaft.*

To think of all peoples on our planet as belonging to the single family of humanity is important. As we move more and more into the post-industrial or communications era, we are becoming aware that decisions on one part of the globe spawn ripples that affect people everywhere else. Localism, parochialism, and even nationalism have become ostrich-ism. We can no longer justify burying our heads in the sand to avoid seeing the need for worldwide cooperation. There is only one future for all people.

The church thinks of itself as catholic. By "catholic" I mean universal, i. e., embracing the saints of every climate and race as well as those of the past and those yet to be born. All are one in Christ. And if the rule of God in his future kingdom is to be complete, then there is no one who will exist outside the divine community. The vision Christians prophesy, then, necessarily conceives of the entire human race as a single *gemeinschaftlich* society. Proleptic action consists in acting to affirm that future unity in the present.

The prophetic visions we project should aim at raising our consciousness of the bond we share with our planetary neighbors. It is not necessary to establish a new world order under a single government at this point; although it is true that the concept of the sovereign nation-state is outmoded. Because of the growth of communications, peoples within the various nations and cultures of the world are beginning to see that their ties to one another and to the future transcend the boundaries set by nationalist politics. This should be further cultivated. As a world consensus begins to develop the individual governments will respond to the global perspective and begin to act in concert with one another. Whatever form of world cooperation develops, it will certainly be a dynamic balance between world unity and local diversity.[17]

§

This suggests the third contribution the church can make to planning for the new world of tomorrow. Both within its own institutional life and in the wider society around, the church should support programs that aim to *protect posterity.* This is an extension of promoting global *Gemeinschaft.* It testifies to the bond we share with all humanity, not just spatially around the world but also temporally through the years.

We have a choice. We may revel for a few short decades in one last gluttonous technological fling, gorging ourselves to oversatiation with the natural fruits of earth; or we may invoke a new sense of ecological thrift and devotion to the welfare of our descendants. The "eat, drink, and be merry for tomorrow our children will die" mentality will leave our progeny with a mother earth stripped of her beauty, robbed of her bountiful resources, failing in her fecund ability to generate more life, and gasping for breath in a pool of pollution. Such is the legacy to be inherited by our children if we do not change our will.

But the concept of catholicity prevents us from forgetting either our forebears or our posterity within the church; it ought to stimulate the same concern for all of humankind.

§

The fourth form of Christian action is to help *produce programs* that embody the values derived from our vision of God's intention for the future. For the most part, Christians have not yet produced enough programs for action that confront the problems posed by future forecasters. The futurists have thrown down the gauntlet: we must make choices and take action, otherwise great evils will thunder down upon us.

How does Christian faith go about programming? There is no one single socio-politico-economic formula for society dictated by the Holy Bible valid for every time and situation in human history. The political ideologies held by Christians should not be fixed or static; no unique program is dictated by the Christian ethic. Rather, everyone who approaches our social responsibilities from a perspective of faith must accept the dynamism and relativity of each new situation. What we are granted is a vision, a symbolic image of the future absolute rule of God's loving will. Any programmatic action evolving out of faith, then, requires an existential application of that vision to the present challenge. We develop programs for each new challenge as we understand that challenge in light of our image of God's future.

One interdenominational task force has begun formulating such a program aimed particularly at the problem of world hunger: it is Bread for the World. Made up primarily of church and political leaders with Eugene Carson Blake as the first president, Bread for the World has argued that beyond private charitable giving Christians should seek to influence the U. S. government. This contention is based on the fact that the U. S. is the single largest food supplier in the world; it is capable not only of alleviating short-term crises but also of developing indigenous technologies for producing more food within the hungry nations themselves. Since 1964 the food assistance given the poorer peoples of the world has steadily declined, just like the moral commitment among Americans to be the catalyst for justice around the globe. Bread for the World has been seeking to enlist grass roots pressure on the American government to make a greater commitment to share the wealth. Finally, in 1976 the congress adopted a policy statement on the "right to food" as a direct result of this pressure. The further challenge is now to see to it that practical measures to implement the policy are taken.

Within the various denominations a great deal of laudable work has been done on the food problem. Through personal contributions and various matching programs, the 7 million Lutherans in America directed over 8 million dollars' worth of aid to the hungry lands of the world in 1974 alone. And because overhead costs were largely absorbed by the already established church administration, nearly 94¢ of every $1.00 contributed actually reached the mouth of a hungry person.

Nevertheless, 8 million dollars is far from enough to meet the needs of the 460 million "permanently hungry" identified by the United Nations in 1974. Much more is needed than just that which can be gathered through charity appeals. Only national policy changes can obtain the economic muscle requisite for facing the issue in a big way. Bread for the World is correct on this point.

Thus, in addition to prayer and personal charitable sharing, Christians need to become citizen advocates. As citizens advocating a fundamentally humane economic policy for sharing the world's wealth, American Christians should be writing their representatives and senators and lobbying for new and vigorous governmental action.

One question often posed to the Bread for the World people is: "The problem of hunger is so complex, so enormous—what reason do we have for hope?" The answer is that Christians do not root their hope only in the latest U. N. projections or some social scientist's analysis of what trends are taking us toward the year 2000. Christians root their hope in God and believe that the future of our one world leads to his kingdom, however and whenever it comes.[18]

Bread for the World sets the prototype for other similar efforts to produce planning programs for the future based on our vision of God's will. It involves a combination of charitable giving that emerges from religious faith plus vigorous political action. It affirms both that the future is ultimately in God's hands and also that we are responsible for what happens. It recognizes that the future is both human and divine.

§

Fifth, the church must *propose alliances between Christians and those non-Christians who also have a positive and holistic vision of a truly human future.* The Christian image of the coming kingdom of

God can certainly endorse the visions and priorities set forth by some of the secular humanists reviewed in this book, such as Charles Reich, Victor Ferkiss, John Platt, Lester Brown, and others. In his encyclical *pacem in terris* Pope John XXIII asked Christians to cooperate with "all men of good will" in working for world peace. The church should seek out and support persons in power of differing persuasions when they plan planetarily, when they seek the transformation of nationalistic foreign policies into a worldwide domestic policy. We should form alliances with whoever shares our commitment to all or any part of our vision of a planetary brotherhood and living at peace with nature.

At the same time the critical power of the Christian vision of God's ultimate future will remind us that all human approximations to it are—though good and meaningful—still provisional and not absolute. We must always be on guard against fanaticism, the unflagging belief in one's own rightness that idolatrously absolutizes one human individual or institution. No present political system or even the church itself should ever be identified with the as yet transcendent kingdom of God. To prematurely claim such ultimacy within the confines of human finitude leads to totalitarianism, a demonic unity at the expense of personal individuality. That which we value now as "right" or "good" is done only in the light of the as yet coming absolute good. The positive trends and plans of the present are provisionally good, that is, dependent for their goodness on the future kingdom of God. Because of this, secular society needs the church. Secular society cannot remain secular—aware of its own preliminary character—without the church as a separate institution to remind the present order of its provisionality. As long as humanism, for example, seeks to ground its ethical vision in people alone, it risks losing the critical distance provided by the transcendent future and instead absolutizes people as they are at present.

Thus, on the one hand, Christian eschatology commits us to the provisional; it commits us to endeavor within the provisional matrix of present human affairs to plan with the tools of *futurum.* On the other hand, eschatology commits us to *adventus,* the absolute future that continually reminds us of the preliminary character of present efforts compared to the radical transformation to be brought about by God's power. It commits us to a future that is both human and divine.

§

Finally, the church must *proclaim pardon*. The vision of the coming kingdom is not only law, i. e., not only the will of God that presents the good and judges the present lack of it. It is also gospel. The solution to the eschatological problem is found not in humanity itself but in God's redemptive action. As the power of the future that every moment releases us from the determining power of the past, God is the necessary condition for achieving transformation. We might also say that in light of the promise bequeathed to us in the resurrection of Jesus Christ, he has also shown himself to be the sufficient condition.

The burden of our errors and evils, though heavy, will not weigh upon us forever. Any disaster we bring upon ourselves will be penultimate, not ultimate. Beyond death there is resurrection. To say that "Christ died for our sins" is to say that God himself passionately shares our every suffering, and that as his incarnate Son passed from death to new life so also does God promise death to the present eon and resurrection to the new one. Suffer and die we must during these birth pangs of the new humanity, but the good news of the gospel message of forgiveness is that the new for which we hope will not ultimately be stillborn. If not *"we"* then certainly *"he* shall overcome." This provides an inner anesthetic for the pains of our present labor. We may have confidence that even when we "sin and fall short of the glory" of the vision of God's kingdom, there is still "mercy without end."

NOTES

Chapter 1. Toward the Year 2000

1. Alvin Toffler, ed., *The Futurists* (New York: Random House, 1972), p. 3.

2. John McHale, *The Future of the Future* (New York: George Braziller, 1969), p. 15.

3. *Ibid.,* p. 5.

4. Robert Theobald, *Beyond Despair* (Washington: New Republic Book Co., 1976), p. 20.

5. Victor Ferkiss, *The Future of Technological Civilization* (New York: George Braziller, 1974), p. 6.

6. Lynn White, Jr., "The Historical Roots of Our Ecological Crisis," *Science,* 10 March 1967, pp. 1203–1207. Reprinted in *The Environmental Handbook,* ed. Garrett de Bell (New York: Ballantine Books, 1970), pp. 12–26.

7. Langdon Gilkey, *Naming the Whirlwind: The Renewal of God-Language* (Indianapolis: The Bobbs-Merrill Co., 1969), p. 280.

8. Paul Tillich, *Theology of Culture* (New York: Oxford University Press, 1959), pp. 7–8; cf. his *Systematic Theology,* 3 vols. (Chicago: University of Chicago Press, 1963), 3:95.

9. Frederick Ferré, *Basic Modern Philosophy of Religion* (New York: Charles Scribner's Sons, 1967), p. 61; and Ferré's *Shaping the Future* (New York: Harper & Row, 1976), p. 9.

10. Tillich, *Systematic Theology,* 2:114–115.

11. Rudolf Bultmann, *Kerygma and Myth,* ed. Hans Werner Bartsch (New York: Harper & Row, 1961), p. 20; and his *Jesus Christ and Mythology* (New York: Charles Scribner's Sons, 1958), p. 81.

12. Karl Barth, *Church Dogmatics,* 4 vols. (Edinburgh: T. & T. Clark, 1956), Vol. I, Part 2, pp. 113–114.

13. Wolfhart Pannenberg, *Theology and the Philosophy of Science* (Philadelphia: The Westminster Press, 1976), p. 281.

14. Charles A. Reich, *The Greening of America* (New York: Bantam Books, 1970), p. 2.

15. Carl Braaten, *Christ and Counter-Christ: Apocalyptic Themes in Theology and Culture* (Philadelphia: Fortress Press, 1972), p. 117.

16. James H. Cone, *A Black Theology of Liberation* (Philadelphia: J. B. Lippincott, 1970), pp. 247–248.

17. Donella H. Meadows, et al., *The Limits to Growth* (New York: Universe Books, 1972). Mihajlo Mesarovic and Eduard Pestel, *Mankind at the Turning Point* (New York: E. P. Dutton, 1974).

18. Alvin Toffler, *Future Shock* (New York: Bantam Books, 1970).

19. Gordon Rattray Taylor, *The Biological Time-Bomb* (New York: Mentor Book, 1969).

20. Johannes B. Metz, *Theology of the World* (New York: Herder and Herder, 1969), esp. chapter 6.

21. R. Buckminster Fuller, *Utopia or Oblivion: The Prospects for Humanity* (New York: Overlook Press, 1969).

22. Carl Braaten, *The Future of God* (New York: Harper & Row, 1969), p. 29 (Braaten's italics); cf. *Christ and Counter-Christ*, p. 11.

23. Karl Rahner, "A Fragmentary Aspect of a Theological Evaluation of the Concept of the Future," *Theological Investigations*, 10 vols. to date (London: Darton, Longman & Todd, 1973), 10:237.

Chapter 2. Millennialist and Apocalyptic Perspectives

1. Hal Lindsey, *The Late Great Planet Earth* (New York: Bantam Books, 1970), p. 33. Note the critical examination of Lindsey's work by Roy A. Harrisville, "Tomorrow with Hal Lindsey," *Dialog* 13, no. 4 (Autumn 1974): 290–296.

2. Lindsey, pp. 32ff.

3. *Ibid.,* p. 126.

4. R. H. Charles, *Eschatology: The Doctrine of a Future Life in Israel, Judaism, and Christianity* (New York: Schocken Books, 1963), p. 248.

5. Walter Schmithals, *The Apocalyptic Movement,* trans. John E. Steely (Nashville: Abingdon Press, 1975), pp. 89–110.

6. *Ibid.,* p. 44.

7. D. S. Russell, *The Method and Message of Jewish Apocalyptic* (Philadelphia: The Westminster Press, 1964), p. 232.

Chapter 3. Christ: The Future Made Present

1. Joachim Jeremias, *The Lord's Prayer* (Philadelphia: Fortress Press Facet Book, 1964), pp. 23ff.

2. R. H. Charles, *Eschatology: The Doctrine of a Future Life,* pp. 19–31.

3. Raymond E. Brown, *The Virginal Conception and Bodily Resurrection of Jesus* (New York: Paulist Press, 1973), pp. 112–113.

4. Willi Marxsen, *The Resurrection of Jesus of Nazareth* (Philadelphia: Fortress Press, 1970), p. 147 (Marxsen's italics).

5. Rudolf Bultmann, "Ist Jesus auferstanden wie Goethe?" *Der Spiegel,* 25 July 1966, pp. 42–45. English translation by Carol Fellows, "An Interview with Rudolf Bultmann," *Christianity and Crisis* 26, 14 November 1966, p. 254. Cf. *Kerygma and Myth,* pp. 41–44.

6. Bultmann, "Is Exegesis without Presuppositions Possible?" in *Existence and Faith,* trans. Schubert Ogden (New York: Meridian Books, 1960), p. 291.

7. Marc Bloch, *The Historian's Craft* (New York: Random House, Vintage Edition, 1953), p. 115.

8. David Hume, *An Enquiry Concerning Human Understanding,* Section X, Part I.

9. Wolfhart Pannenberg, *Jesus, God and Man,* trans. Lewis L. Wilkins and Duane A. Priebe (Philadelphia: The Westminster Press, 1968), p. 105. See also Pannenberg's critique of the analogy principle in *Basic Questions in Theology,* 2 vols. (Philadelphia: Fortress Press, 1970–71), 1:39–53.

10. This point is the emphasis of George Nichelsburg in his thorough study of *Resurrection, Immortality, and Eternal Life in Intertestamental Judaism,* Harvard Theological Studies, vol. 26 (Cambridge, Mass.: Harvard University Press, 1972).

11. Paul Scherer, *The Word God Sent* (New York: Harper & Row, 1965), p. 32.

12. Jürgen Moltmann, *Hope and Planning* (New York: Harper & Row, 1971), p. 43; cf. *Religion, Revolution, and the Future* (New York: Charles Scribner's Sons, 1969), pp. 45, 61–62.

13. Moltmann, *Hope and Planning,* p. 42; cf. *The Crucified God* (New York: Harper & Row, 1974), pp. 174–178.

Chapter 4. Hope in the Future

1. Reich, *The Greening of America,* p. 418.

2. Robert Heilbroner, *An Inquiry into the Human Prospect* (New York: W. W. Norton & Co., 1974), chapter 1.

3. See Russell B. Norris, *God, Marx, and the Future: Dialogue with Roger Garaudy* (Philadelphia: Fortress Press, 1974), pp. 22–24.

4. Roger Garaudy, *Humanisme Marxiste* (Paris: Editions Sociales, 1967), p. 58. Cited by Norris, *God, Marx, and the Future,* p. 24.

5. Wolfhart Pannenberg, "Can Christianity Do without an Eschatology?" in G. B. Caird et al., *The Christian Hope,* Theological Collections, vol. 13 (London: S. P. C. K., 1970), p. 29; cf. Pannenberg's *Theology and the Kingdom of God* (Philadelphia: The Westminster Press, 1969), pp. 81–82.

6. Daniel J. Boorstin, *The Image: A Guide to Pseudo-Events in America* (New York: Harper & Row, Colophon Book, 1962), p. 7.

7. Toffler, *Future Shock,* p. 52.

8. Fuller, *Utopia or Oblivion,* p. 286.

9. Karl Marx, "Critique of the Gotha Programme," *Basic Writings on Politics and Philosophy* by Karl Marx and Friedrich Engels (New York: Doubleday Anchor Book, 1959), p. 119.

10. John Maynard Keynes, "Economic Possibilities for Our Grandchildren," *Essays in Persuasion* (New York: Harcourt, Brace and Co., 1932), pp. 364–365.

11. Daniel Bell, *The Coming of Post-Industrial Society* (New York: Basic Books, 1973), p. 117.

12. Herman Kahn and Anthony J. Wiener, "The Next Thirty-Three Years: A Framework for Speculation," *Toward the Year 2000: Work in Progress*, ed. Daniel Bell (Boston: Beacon Press, 1967), p. 85. For an update, see Kahn's article with William Brown, "And a Better Prospect for the Future," *The Futurist* 9, no. 6 (December 1975): 285, and Kahn's *The Next 200 Years* (New York: William Morrow and Co., 1976), pp. 48–49, 130, 209.

13. John R. Platt, *The Step to Man* (New York: John Wiley & Sons, 1966), p. 166.

14. *Ibid.*, p. 161.

15. *Ibid.*, p. 157. The publication date of Platt's book is 1966, just about the time American soldiers were pushing captured members of the Viet Cong out the doors of flying helicopters and William Calley was slaughtering women and children at My Lai. Have we really become more humane?

16. *Ibid.*, p. 202.

17. *Ibid.*, p. 168.

18. Victor Ferkiss, *Technological Man* (New York: Mentor Book, 1969); and *The Future of Technological Civilization*, pp. 88–89, 206ff., 264.

19. Bell, *The Coming of Post-Industrial Society*, pp. 14ff., 348ff., 378ff.

20. Ferkiss, *Technological Man*, pp. 35–36.

21. Hans Schwarz, *On the Way to the Future* (Minneapolis, Minn.: Augsburg Publishing House, 1972), p. 22.

22. Erich Fromm, *The Revolution of Hope* (New York: Harper & Row, 1968), p. 13.

23. Thomas J. Cottle and Stephen L. Klineberg, *The Present of Things Future* (New York: Free Press, 1974), p. 21.

24. Cone, *A Black Theology of Liberation*, p. 248.

25. Ernst Bloch, *Das Prinzip Hoffnung*, 3 vols. (Frankfurt: Suhrkamp Verlag, 1959), 3:1202. Cited in Braaten, *The Future of God*, p. 38. Of course, Bloch, who sees hope as an essential ingredient in his Marxism, is not content to leave us thinking he is going to remain simply religious. He argues that we have advanced beyond the superstitious constructs within which hope was originally cast, so that as atheists with a "meta-religious consciousness" we can remove God as the object of our hope and replace him with our own perfection. Cf. Bloch, *Man on His Own* (New York: Herder and Herder, 1970), pp. 160ff. He too ends up with the eschatological problem.

26. Braaten, *The Future of God*, p. 38.

27. Rahner, *Theological Investigations*, 10:261–262.

28. Fromm, *Revolution of Hope*, p. 13.

Chapter 5. Time and History

1. Platt, *The Step to Man*, p. 185.

2. Toffler, *Future Shock*, p. 1.

3. *Ibid.*, p. 11.

4. Meadows et al., *The Limits to Growth*. The authors used the computer-science

approach of the MIT professor Jay Forrester: see his *World Dynamics* (Cambridge, Mass.: Wright-Allen Press, 1971).

5. Since the publication of *The Limits to Growth* the Club of Rome has backed off somewhat on its use of the *world* model. Cf. Jay Forrester, "The Road to World Harmony," *The Futurist* 9 (October 1975): 231–234. Forrester's new emphasis on local communities and individual countries is directed toward the need for them to initiate remedial action, simply because there is at present no single worldwide political organization capable of solving the world's problems. However, he has not given up his contention that our problems are basically global in scope and that our ultimate goal is *"world* harmony" (italics mine). Cf. also Mesarovic and Pestel, *Mankind at the Turning Point,* pp. 5, 20, 31.

6. Kenneth Vaux, ed., *To Create a Different Future: Religious Hope and Technological Planning* (New York: Friendship Press, 1972), p. 13. Herman Kahn is highly critical of the limits-to-growth scenario; cf. *The Next 200 Years,* pp. 20, 49ff., 62, 84, 88–93, 113–114, 121–122, 165–166, 199, and 210–211.

7. Lester R. Brown, "Global Food Insecurity," *The Futurist* 8, no. 2 (April 1974): 59.

8. *Ibid.,* p. 60. Cf. Brown and Erik P. Eckholm, "Let Them Eat Bread," *The Humanist* 34, no. 6 (November/December 1974): 6–10.

9. Lester R. Brown, "Defusing the Population Timebomb," *The Christian Century* 91, no. 29 (August 21–28, 1974): 792. Cf. also Brown's *By Bread Alone* (New York: Praeger Publishers, 1974).

10. Paul Ehrlich, "Eco-catastrophe," *The Futurists,* ed. Toffler, p. 23.

11. Mircea Eliade, *The Sacred and the Profane* (New York: Harcourt, Brace & World, 1959), p. 73.

12. *Akitu* is described by Helmer Ringgren, *Religions of the Ancient Near East* (Philadelphia: The Westminster Press, 1973), pp. 83–89, and by Henri Frankfort, *Kingship and the Gods* (Chicago: University of Chicago Press, 1948), pp. 313–333.

13. June Goodfield and Stephen Toulmin, *The Discovery of Time* (London: Hutchinson, 1965), p. 33. Cf. also Roger L. Shinn's article, "Augustinian and Cyclical Views of History," *Anglican Theological Review* 31 (July 1949): 133–141.

14. Mircea Eliade, *Cosmos and History: The Myth of the Eternal Return* (New York: Harper Torchbook, 1959), p. 52.

15. Ferkiss, *Technological Man,* pp. 22, 43–44.

16. Henri Yaker et al., eds., *The Future of Time* (Garden City, N. Y.: Doubleday, 1971), p. 24.

17. Pannenberg, *Basic Questions in Theology,* 1:18.

18. Gerhard von Rad, *Old Testament Theology,* 2 vols. (Edinburgh: Oliver & Boyd; and New York: Harper & Row, 1962–65), 2:115.

19. Edmond Jacob, *Theology of the Old Testament* (New York: Harper & Brothers, 1958), pp. 188–189.

20. Jürgen Moltmann, *The Theology of Hope* (New York: Harper & Row, 1967), pp. 103–106.

21. G. van der Leeuw, "Primordial Time and Final Time," *Man and Time,* vol. 3

of the Eranos Yearbooks (New York: Pantheon, 1957), p. 340. Cf. also Mircea Eliade, *Cosmos and History*, p. vii.

22. Rudolf Bultmann, *History and Eschatology* (New York: Harper Torchbook, 1957), p. 70.

23. The German philosopher Karl Löwith writes, "modern historical consciousness has discarded the Christian faith in a central event of absolute relevance, yet it maintains its logical antecedents and consequences, viz., the past as preparation and the future as consummation, thus reducing the history of salvation to the impersonal teleology of a progressive evolution in which every present stage is the fulfillment of past preparations." *Meaning in History* (Chicago: University of Chicago Press, 1949), p. 186.

24. Eliade, *The Sacred and the Profane*, pp. 95–99.

25. Gilles Quispel writes, "In the New Testament man stands in a process which draws its meaning and virtue from an invisible end; mankind, and the cosmos as well, has an *eschaton*, a *telos*, an end which draws events toward it like a magnet." "Time and History in Patristic Christianity," *Man and Time*, p. 86.

26. On the context of meaning see Wilhelm Dilthey, *Pattern and Meaning in History* (New York: Harper & Row, 1961), p. 106, and Pannenberg, *Basic Questions in Theology*, 1:98–99, 162–163; 2:61–62; *Theology and the Philosophy of Science*, pp. 129, 216, 284.

27. Fred Polak, *The Image of the Future*, trans. and abridged by Elise Boulding (New York: Elsevier Scientific Publishing Co., 1973), p. 19.

28. Heilbroner, *An Inquiry into the Human Prospect*, p. 126.

Chapter 6. Values for a Planetary Society

1. Toffler, ed., *The Futurists*, p. 3.

2. Toffler, *Future Shock*, p. 486; see p. 35. Toffler makes this same point in his introductory essay to *Values and the Future*, ed. Kurt Baier and Nicholas Rescher (New York: Free Press, 1969), pp. 18–19.

3. Reich, *The Greening of America*, p. 13. The understanding-decision-control formula was the point of the opening address by Roy Amara at the Second General Assembly of the World Future Society on June 2, 1975. See *The Next 25 Years: Crises and Opportunities*, ed. Andrew A. Spekke (Washington: World Future Society, 1975), pp. 1–5.

4. Meadows et al., *The Limits to Growth*, p. 11; cf. pp. 86, 181.

5. *Ibid.*, p. 181.

6. *Ibid.*, p. 150.

7. *Ibid.*, pp. 68, 85–86, 181–182. It was the demand for decision that provoked the title of the Club of Rome's second book: *Mankind at the Turning Point*.

8. Lester R. Brown, *In the Human Interest: A Strategy to Stabilize World Population* (New York: W. W. Norton & Co., 1974).

9. Brown, "Defusing the Population Timebomb," *The Christian Century* 91, no. 29 (August 21–28, 1974): 795.

10. Marshall McLuhan, *Understanding Media: The Extensions of Man* (New York: New American Library Signet Edition, 1964), p. 19. McLuhan here is in agreement with the spectrum of future-oriented sociology. Cf. Ferkiss, *Technological Man*, p. 75.

11. Fuller, *Utopia or Oblivion*, p. 275. The economic and cultural pressures toward a planetary society are more thoroughly presented by John McHale, *The Future of the Future*, especially chapter VI; by Victor Ferkiss, *The Future of Technological Civilization*, pp. 193–206; and by Mesarovic and Pestel, *Mankind at the Turning Point*, chapter 3.

12. John Kenneth Galbraith, *Economics and the Public Purpose* (Boston: Houghton Mifflin Co., 1973), pp. 164–175.

13. For an example of the lack of common sense on the issue see Ferré, *Shaping the Future*, pp. 169–173.

14. Richard Post, "A Permanent and Limitless Energy Source for the World," *Center Report* 5, no. 4 (October 1972): 9.

15. Margaret Mead, "Ways to Deal with the Current Social Transformation," *The Futurist* 8, no. 3 (June 1974): 123.

16. Ervin Laszlo, *A Strategy for the Future* (New York: George Braziller, 1974), p. 112.

17. Kenneth Boulding, "The Economics of the Coming Spaceship Earth," *The Futurists*, ed. Alvin Toffler, p. 236.

18. Platt, *The Step to Man*, p. 200.

19. *Ibid.*, p. 202.

20. *Ibid.*, p. 203.

21. John R. Platt, "What We Must Do," *Science*, 28 November 1969, p. 1115; cf. his "The Future of Social Crises" in *The Next 25 Years*, pp. 6–9.

22. Fuller, *Utopia or Oblivion*, p. 291.

23. Platt, *The Step to Man*, p. 203.

24. Heilbroner, *An Inquiry into the Human Prospect*, p. 143.

25. *Ibid.*, p. 115.

26. Daniel Bell, "The Year 2000—The Trajectory of an Idea," *Toward the Year 2000*, p. 8 (italics mine).

27. Garrett Hardin, "The Tragedy of the Commons," *Science*, 13 December 1968, p. 1243. Cited in *The Limits to Growth*, p. 150.

28. Bell, *The Coming of Post-Industrial Society*, p. 364.

29. Herman Kahn and Anthony J. Wiener, "The Next Thirty-Three Years," *Toward the Year 2000*, p. 95.

30. Bell, *The Coming of Post-Industrial Society*, p. 480. Cf. the discussion on pp. 477–480.

31. Ferkiss, *Technological Man*, p. 187.

32. *Ibid.*, p. 197.

33. *Ibid.*, p. 222.

34. *Ibid.*, p. 203.

35. *Ibid.*, pp. 27–32.

36. Victor Ferkiss, "Christianity, Technology and the Human Future," *Dialog* 13, no. 4 (Autumn 1974): 262; cf. *The Future of Technological Civilization.*

37. Ferkiss, *The Future of Technological Civilization,* pp. 134ff.

38. John R. Platt, "World Transformation: Changes in Belief Systems," *The Futurist* 8, no. 3 (June 1974): 124.

39. *Ibid.,* p. 125.

Chapter 7. The Humanist Alternative

1. John Julian Ryan, *The Humanization of Man* (New York: Paulist/Newman Press, 1972), p. 6.

2. Reich, *The Greening of America,* p. 19.

3. *Humanist Manifestos I and II* (Buffalo: Promotheus Books, 1973).

4. Charles Hartshorne, *Beyond Humanism* (Lincoln: University of Nebraska Press, 1968; first published in 1937), p. 13. Karl Rahner would add, "history itself must have an ultimate meaning if the ethical is to have it as well." See: "Christianity and the New Earth" in *Knowledge and the Future of Man,* ed. Walter J. Ong (New York: Simon & Schuster, 1968), p. 267.

5. Paul Tillich, *Dynamics of Faith* (New York: Harper & Row, 1957), pp. 11–12, 97; and *Systematic Theology,* 2:49–51.

6. Hartshorne, *Beyond Humanism,* p. 18.

7. *Ibid.,* p. 19.

8. Ferré, *Shaping the Future,* p. 89.

9. V. F. Calverton, *The Passing of the Gods* (New York: Charles Scribner's Sons, 1934), Preface; cited in Hartshorne, *Beyond Humanism,* p. 2.

10. White, "The Historical Roots of Our Ecological Crisis," *Science* 10 March 1967, pp. 1203–1207. Reprinted in *The Environmental Handbook.*

11. Ian L. McHarg, *Design with Nature* (Garden City, N. Y.: The Natural History Press, 1969), p. 26. See the criticism of this position offered by James Limburg, "What Does It Mean to 'Have Dominion over the Earth'?" in *Dialog* 10, no. 3 (Summer 1971): 221–223. The essence of Limburg's argument is repeated here.

12. Words reprinted from *Thoughts for Everyday Living* by Maltbie D. Babcock; copyright 1901, by Charles Scribner's Sons, 1929, by Katharine T. Babcock. Used by permission of Charles Scribner's Sons.

13. Tillich, *Theology of Culture,* pp. 7–8; cf. *Systematic Theology,* 3:95.

14. Paul B. Horton and Chester L. Hunt, *Sociology,* 3d ed. (New York: McGraw-Hill Book Co., 1972), pp. 86–88.

Chapter 8. Toward a Proleptic Theology of the Future

1. Braaten, *The Future of God,* p. 68.

2. Pierre Teilhard de Chardin, *The Future of Man* (New York: Harper & Row Torchbook, 1969), pp. 124–125.

3. Ferkiss, *The Future of Technological Civilization,* p. 159.

4. Pannenberg, *Theology and the Kingdom of God,* p. 56. Cf. *Basic Questions in Theology,* 2:240; E. Frank Tupper, *The Theology of Wolfhart Pannenberg*

(Philadelphia: The Westminster Press, 1973), pp. 198–203; and Carl Braaten and Robert Jenson, *The Futurist Option* (New York: Paulist/Newman Press, 1970), pp. 26–29.

Chapter 9. Concluding Nonscientific Prescript

1. Moltmann, *Hope and Planning,* p. 178.
2. Hans Küng, *On Being a Christian* (New York: Doubleday, 1976), p. 222.
3. Johannes B. Metz, *Theology of the World,* p. 150; cf. Braaten, *The Future of God,* chapter 5.
4. Langdon Gilkey, *Catholicism Confronts Modernity* (New York: Seabury Press, 1975), p. 133.
5. Pannenberg, *Theology and the Kingdom of God,* p. 111.
6. Karl Marx, "Contribution to the Critique of Hegel's Philosophy of Right," *On Religion* by Karl Marx and Friedrich Engels (New York: Schocken Books, 1964), p. 42 (Marx's italics).
7. Harvey Cox, "The Future of Christianity and the Church," *The Futurist* 4, no. 4 (August 1970): 124.
8. From *The Spirituals and the Blues* by James H. Cone. © 1972 by James H. Cone. Used by permission of Seabury Press.
9. *Ibid.,* p. 95; cf. *A Black Theology of Liberation,* p. 11.
10. Braaten, *Christ and Counter-Christ,* p. 117.
11. Braaten, *The Future of God,* pp. 143–144; *Christ and Counter-Christ,* pp. 104–107. Fred L. Polak agrees. "The specifically Jewish apocalyptic character of the Marxian image of the future is easily recognizable in the doctrine of necessary suffering. The dispossessed and downtrodden workers are the chosen ones, predestined to be elevated. . . . In general it can be said that Marxian thought contains a religious image of the future in secularized form." *The Image of the Future,* p. 122.
12. Polak, *The Image of the Future.*
13. Bell, *The Coming of Post-Industrial Society,* p. 433.
14. Herman Kahn et al., *The Next 200 Years,* p. 210.
15. Kenneth Cauthen, *Christian Biopolitics* (Nashville: Abingdon Press, 1971), p. 47.
16. See the sensitive study of this theme of eating and sharing in Monika K. Hellwig's *The Eucharist and the Hunger of the World* (New York: Paulist Press, 1976).
17. Ervin Laszlo develops this strategy in greater detail. Cf. *A Strategy for the Future.*
18. Arthur Simon, *Bread for the World* (New York: Paulist Press, 1975), p. 140.

INDEX